Nancy Cornwell's

Fl 90-Minute eece

45 Projects for Beginners and Busy Sewers

©2006 Nancy Cornwell
Published by

kp **krause publications**
An Imprint of F+W Publications

700 East State Street • Iola, WI 54990-0001
715-445-2214 • 888-457-2873
www.krausebooks.com

Various products used throughout this book carry specific copyright or trademark symbols. They are:

Faux Chenille® (Nanette Holmberg)
Mesh Transfer Canvas (Clover Needlecraft, Inc.)
Water-Soluble Pencils (Clover Needlecraft, Inc.)
Wash-Away Wonder Tape (W.H. Collins, Inc.)
Chenille by the Inch™ (Fabric Café™)
Husqvarna Viking
Olfa® Chenille Cutter (Olfa – North America)
Olfa® Decorative Wave Blade (Olfa – North America)
Olfa® Decorative Scallop Blade (Olfa – North America)
Olfa® Decorative Pinking Blade (Olfa – North America)
Olfa® Rotary Cutter (Olfa – North America)
June Tailor® Fancy Fleece™ Slotted Ruler (June Tailor, Inc.)
Lycra™ (DuPont Company)
Polarfleece® (Malden Mills Industries, Inc.)
Polartec®
Pooh™, registered by Disney Enterprises Inc.
Nordic®
Nordic fleece™ (David Textiles, Inc.)
Omnistrips™ (Omnigrid®, Inc.)
Fasturn® (the Crowning Touch, Inc.)
The Snap Source®
The SnapSetter® (The Snap Source®)

Whenever brand-name products are mentioned, it is because I have personally used them and been pleased with the results. In this day and age, with new products constantly being introduced, there may be other comparable products.

Library of Congress Catalog Number: 2006929415
ISBN 13: 978-0-89689-408-2
ISBN 10: 0-89689-408-8

Edited by Maria L. Turner • Designed by Katie Newby
Printed in the United States of America

❧dedication

To Evelyn Grace, my first grandchild, who has blessed my life with a new wonder and appreciation of all that can be.

Both Evelyn Plein and Grace Cornwell were honored in the Dedication of my very first book, Adventures With Polarfleece: *Evelyn, my mom, because she was a strong woman, who, before it was fashionable, instilled* in me the belief that I could accomplish anything to which I set my mind and heart; Grace, my mother-in-law; without her tremendous love and support, the fabric store Jeff and I owned and all the books that followed never would have become a reality.

I hope someday Evelyn Grace feels the same way about me.

❧acknowledgments

The world of fleece sewing has certainly changed since I wrote my first book, *Adventures With Polarfleece*, in 1997. If anyone would have told me where this adventure would lead, I would have laughed and never believed them.

So much of the growth and popularity of fleece has come from the creativity of many people in the sewing industry who continually offer new products that allow imaginations to run wild.

My heartfelt thanks go to:

• David Textiles, Inc. for its ongoing line of high-quality Nordic Fleece in phenomenal prints and colors that keep the imagination working overtime. (Without David Textiles' fleece, there never would have been this series of books.) Also, the garments and blankets featured in this book were made using Nordic Fleece manufactured by David Textiles, Inc. I choose this fleece because I can count on its consistent high quality and know it is readily available through all fabric shops. If your local fabric store doesn't carry Nordic Fleece, ask the owner or manager to order it for you.

• Sue Hausmann and Husqvarna Viking for their continual support of my ongoing fleece adventure and for providing me with a Designer SE to sew all the models featured throughout the book. I admire Husqvarna Viking's mission to "Keep the World Sewing." Their innovative machine, products and education continually expand the sewing horizon.

• Sew 'n' Sew (an excellent Husqvarna Viking dealer in Waupaca, Wis.), with special thanks to owners Bonnie and Sam Welsch for the generous loan of their "personal" Designer SE for photography throughout the book.

• Olfa – North America for its decorative blades and new Chenille Cutter. As you go through the book, it is obvious I am in love with these innovative sewing tools. Carl Cottrell, vice president of marketing – North America, has enthusiastically supported all my fleece endeavors and listened to my opinions. (Thanks for the decorative scallop blade, Carl.)

• Clover Needlecraft, Inc. for its Mesh Transfer Canvas and water-soluble pencils. I will forever be grateful to Clover for these products, as they provide the easiest way to mark and transfer designs onto fleece. Many people ask why I didn't mention them in my very first book. They weren't on the market yet! A special thanks to Jan Carr and Syl Pearson on keeping me current on the new products.

• Editor Maria Turner, photographers Robert Best and Kris Kandler, illustrator Rachael Knier, photo stylist Mary Collette and book designer Katie Newby for taking my writing, rough sketches and concepts and making them look good "in print."

• Jeff, my husband and the most important person to thank, as without his steady and constant support, encouragement, patience and understanding, none of my books would have ever come to life. You are truly my best friend and "the wind beneath my wings."

table of contents

fleece projects

section
two

fleece for adults

fleece for the outdoors

fleece for the home

Fleece is perfect fit for Halloween

Fall is a very heavy travel season for me. So when my granddaughter, Evelyn, was a couple of weeks old, my son, Jeff, and I were discussing what she would be for Halloween. Knowing how hectic my schedule was, Jeff said he'd buy her costume, rather than ask me to make one. But at the end of October, I got a frantic call on my cell phone.

Jeff: "They don't make Halloween costumes for 2-month-olds!"

Me: "I know. That's why I asked you about a costume a couple weeks ago."

Jeff: "Oh. Well, change of plans."

Me: "OK."

Jeff: "Evelyn is going to be a piece of candy corn."

Me (thinking 'Candy Cornwell?'): "OK."

Jeff: "Where are you?"

Me: "Houston."

Jeff: "When are you coming home?"

Me: "The night before Halloween."

Jeff: "This conversation is kind of a moot point, isn't it?"

Me: "Kinda."

Jeff: "Do you have white, yellow and orange fleece? I can make it!"

So, Jeff, my 30-year-old-son who virtually grew up in our fabric store, raided my fleece supply. He laid Evelyn on my cutting table, drew a triangle around her on pattern tracing material, divided the triangle into thirds and made his 2-month-old baby girl her very first Halloween costume... And it was precious.

After listening to me for so many years, he knew to lengthen his stitch length. He knew he could just cut out the face opening and armholes because fleece doesn't ravel. He even put the Snap Source's sport snaps along the bottom edge. However, as you can see by the photo, Evelyn was not impressed with her dad's sewing prowess or creativity — and no way were those snaps going to be snapped!

intro

Calling this book 90-Minute Fleece is a subjective, rather than definitive, time-frame statement. Everyone sews at her own pace. Some sewers have a "close counts" attitude, toss their fleece on the cutting table, cut and sew. Other sewers are precise and take as much time for the layout and cutting prep as they do for the construction.

The 90-minute "quick-sew" designation applies to the construction aspects of each project. And again, some sewers are pedal-to-the-metal and quick to the finish, while others take their time, get creative, add embellishments and enjoy the journey.

The projects offered here are not massively time-consuming. They are projects that can be made in an evening. The only blatant exception to the project-in-an-evening concept is the Dramatic Chenille Cape. It's just so eye-catching and show-stopping that I had to include it.

Although the projects are categorized as those for babies, kids, adults, outdoors or your home, realize that with a print choice and/or dimension change, virtually every project could cross over from kids to home decor to babies to adults.

All of the techniques used in this book have been featured in depth in one of my previous books. I include technique information in this book, but I will also reference my other books if you want more in-depth guidance.

Since the concept of this book is quick and easy, I've included a multisized vest pattern at the back of the book. It is sized for children and ladies, so you won't even have to take the time to dig through your pattern stash trying to decide which pattern to use.

I hope you enjoy using my fleece techniques as much as I enjoy presenting them to you.

Love,

Nancy Cornwell

A happier Candy Corn Evelyn joins friends Pooh Bryce Cranmore and Lion Jordan Artherholt to celebrate everyone's first Halloween.

tips, tools & techniques

the most important thing to remember

When I present seminars across the country, I am frequently asked, "What's the most important thing to remember when sewing on fleece?

The answer is easy, and always the same: Lengthen your stitch length … always … on both your sewing machine and serger.

The No. 1 problem when sewing with fleece, if there is a problem, is a stitch length that is too short.

- If your seams or hems are wavy, your stitch length is too short.
- If your buttonholes pucker and "frogmouth," your stitch length is too short.
- If your appliqués have rippled edges, your stitch length is too short.
- If your pintucked "polar ribbing" is wavy, your stitch length is too short.
- If your zippers buckle, you didn't use Wonder Tape to hold it in place and… your stitch length is too short.

Fleece is a very cooperative and forgiving fabric with which to sew. It just doesn't want a lot of stitches and thread jam-packed into the fabric.

I love how I explained this in my *More Polar Magic* book, so I'll repeat myself:

Remember Ruffled Rib

Using a ruffled rib on the edges of fleece creates a frilly and feminine look when done on purpose, but be aware that a stitch length that is too short also will create this same look— unintentionally—on hems, seams, zippers, pockets and buttonholes.

If you think about the logic behind using a longer stitch length, you will never again forget to lengthen the stitch length. It really makes sense.

Remember how we used to make ruffled rib trim—that frilly, lettuce-edged finish on ribbing collars and cuffs? To get the rippled effect, you hold the folded edge of the ribbing between both hands, pull the ribbing taut and zigzag stitch over the edge, using a wide, dense satin stitch. In reality, you are sewing incorrectly for a purpose.

You stretch the ribbing and cover the edge with stitches so when you let go of the stretched ribbing, it cannot bounce back to its original dimension because there is too much thread piled in. The result is a distorted, wavy edge. On ribbing, it ruffles and looks pretty. On fleece garments (or any knit garment), it manifests itself in wavy hems, buckled zippers, rippled appliqués and more.

Ribbing is a stretch fabric, and so is fleece. The same thing happens if you use a too-short stitch length when sewing hems, seams, zippers, pockets or buttonholes. If you force in too much thread (too many stitches), the fleece will stretch and wave. It's pretty when making ruffled rib… not pretty in garment construction!

nancy's golden rule

Always lengthen your stitch length—on both your sewing machine and serger.

Lengthen the stitch length to at least 3mm. (That's about nine stitches per inch.)

Personally, I sew with a 3.5mm or 4mm stitch length when sewing on fleece.

fabric and garment care

Pre-treating

There's no need to pre-launder fleece since it does not shrink or shed excess color. You can buy it and sew immediately!

Laundering

To avoid unnecessary abrasion, wash finished garments inside-out and with similar garments. Use warm water and a gentle cycle.

Don't use bleach or softening agents (liquid or dryer sheets).

Hang to dry or toss in the dryer on low heat for a short time to relax any wrinkles occurring from the washer spin cycle.

Pressing

Do not iron fleece. Never place an iron soleplate in direct contact with fleece. Direct contact with an iron may leave a permanent iron imprint on the nap of the fleece.

If you feel a compelling urge to press (to encourage a seam to lay flat or relax a wrinkle), hold the iron above the fleece and steam it. Then gently finger-press to encourage the fleece to lay in the desired position.

Which is the Right Side?

To find the right side of fleece, stretch it on the crossgrain (selvage to selvage, which is the direction of the most stretch) along the cut edge. The fleece will curl to the wrong side.

Remember this trick: You will use it often.

nancy's notes

Laundering

I am careful not to launder fleece with garments or fabrics that shed a lot of lint (garments that leave a layer of lint in the lint trap). Things like towels, cotton underwear, etc. The polyester nap of fleece tends to grab onto and hold lint (looking like a facial tissue inadvertently sneaked into the dryer).

The Right Side

Many times you will handle a small piece of fleece (a square, a patch or an appliqué), and you won't have a selvage edge to refer to. So how do you find the crossgrain in order to find the right side of the fabric? Gently stretch the cut edges of the piece. The edge with the most stretch is the crossgrain. After determining the cut edge with the most stretch, tug along that cut edge and the fleece will curl to the wrong side.

general sewing basics

Machine Maintenance

Make sure your sewing machine and serger are cleaned, oiled and in good working order. Sewing with fleece results in a lot of lint, so clean your machines frequently and oil according to the directions in your owner's manual.

Thread

Choose good-quality, long-staple polyester thread that matches your fleece color or is a shade darker. Don't be tempted by bargain threads, as they fray and break easily. They're not worth the hassle.

Needles

Always begin each project with a fresh, new needle.

Because fleece is a knitted fabric, choose a universal, stretch or ball-point needle. These needles have rounded points that deflect, rather than pierce, the yarn.

Choose needle size 70/10 or 75/11 for lightweight fleece, 80/12 or 90/14 for mid-weight fleece, or 100/16 for heavyweight fleece.

Fabric

For more in-depth fleece fabric information and fleece construction techniques, please refer to my *Adventures With Polarfleece* book.

A Note About Fabric Width Variances

Fleece "cutable" widths can vary from 58" to 62" and still be classified as 60" fabric on the bolt end. Many things affect the finished dimension of the fleece fabric: minor (but varying) differences in the yarns used, the tension on the knitting machine, dyestuffs, humidity or variances in the finishing process. All are minor things, but they cause enough variance for one fleece to offer 58" cutable width (after removing the selvages), while the next one offers 62".

Always measure your fleece's "cutable width" when cutting quilt blocks that use the full 60". If your fleece is a little narrower, adjust your block sizes a little to accommodate the fleece width. A square ¼" narrower is certainly not going to affect the visual appearance of a blanket.

As the old (but wise) home decorating adage says: *Measure twice and cut once.*

Other Basic Notions Needed

Scissors
45mm rotary cutter
Cutting mat
Ruler
Tape measure

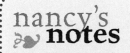

nancy's notes

Thread

Since the stitches will sink into the loft of fleece, a matching thread color is not critical.
If I don't have a good match on hand, I choose something that blends easily.

Black or navy thread works great on any dark-colored fleece, medium gray blends with mid-tones and white or cream goes well with pastels.

Needles

It never fails to amaze me how many "machine problems" are corrected by a simple needle change.
If you experience noisy stitching, change your needle. It's dull or bent.
If you experience skipped stitches or broken needles, go up one needle size. It's too lightweight for the job.
If you experience broken threads, change the needle. It is dull or bent.
If you still experience broken threads (even with a fresh needle), check your throat plate and bobbin shuttle face for rough edges. (Nicks and/or burrs are a fact of life when sewing. You break a needle. It happens. It broke because it hit something metal and left a rough edge. You can use a fine crocus cloth to smooth small rough spots. For bad gouges, let your machine dealer mechanic handle them.)
If you are using an older, temperamental machine and experience skipped stitches, try using a zigzag stitch that is 3mm to 4mm long and .5mm to 1mm wide.

gotta-have notions

References

Referencing my previous books shows an obviously biased opinion. Still, each book offers a different perspective on sewing with fleece and the continued response from sewers indicate they "fit the bill." So...

Adventures with Polarfleece®

This award-winning book has been acknowledged as the sewing industry's "polar encyclopedia." It features in-depth information on everyday sewing and construction techniques on fleece for sewing machines and sergers. Also detailed: No-hassle zipper insertions; buttonholes (standard, fashion and trouble-shooting); ready-to-wear edge finishes; how to choose patterns; and much more.

More Polarfleece® Adventures

This book focuses on surface embellishment without an embroidery machine—pure and simple playing. Sculpturing, double-needle sculpturing, pintucking, cutwork, appliqué and more edge finishes and buttonhole options also are detailed.

Polar Magic

This award-winning book introduces "crossover" sewing, which is incorporating traditionally nonfleece techniques into everyday fleece sewing. There are trapunto, chenille, embossing, pintucking, machine embroidery and various appliqué techniques. It also features an in-depth chapter on polar ribbing. Great home dec ideas are included.

More Polar Magic

You'll find greatly expanded fleece techniques, building on techniques from earlier books, plus new options. It features a large chapter on chenille and chenille strips and includes a multisized jacket pattern for making the jacket featured on the cover, plus three variations.

Embroidery Machine Essentials: Fleece Techniques

Using fleece as a canvas for machine embroidery opens up a whole new world for creativity. First learn a variety of methods for successful embroidery on fleece and then discover how to extract "hidden designs" from each motif. Apply this approach to your embroidery library and each design's potential grows exponentially! This book includes a CD with 20 exclusive, original designs.

Wash-Away Wonder Tape

I have recommended this ¼"-wide double-sided basting tape in all my books. I choose this basting tape for three important reasons:

- It has terrific holding power.
- You can sew through it without gumming up the needle.
- It washes away in the first laundering.

Look for the words "wash-away" to be sure you have the correct product.

It is perfect for aligning and holding project pieces in place where pins might allow shifting. It is the only way to "baste" zippers and pockets in place—on fleece or *any* fabric!

Water-Soluble Pencils

Clover Water-Soluble Pencils *easily* mark on fleece and *stay marked* until erased with water or rubbed away. I find other marking tools are either too difficult to see, or they rub off too easily when handling the fabric.

Caution: Sharpen these pencils only to a medium point, as an over-sharpened point breaks too easily.

Mesh Transfer Canvas

This handy notion from Clover makes transferring designs and motifs onto fleece—or anything—a very simple process. Mesh Transfer Canvas is a 12" x 16" piece of fine-gauge plastic mesh. It has the benefit of being reusable. Trace the design using a water-soluble or regular pencil if you want to reuse the canvas. Use a permanent pen if you want the traced mesh to serve as a permanent template.

Here's how:

1. Lay the transfer canvas over the motif and trace with a water-soluble pencil.

2. Lay the traced mesh canvas on your fleece and redraw the design again with a water-soluble pencil.

The pencil marks go through the mesh holes, easily transferring the design onto the fleece. It's quick and easy!

nancy's note

There is a shiny side and a matte side on Clover Mesh Transfer Canvas. I find it much easier to see my traced lines when I draw on the matte side.

Rotary Cutters

There are a variety of good rotary cutters on the market. While the standard 45mm blade size works just fine, I prefer to use the larger 60mm size. The larger blade effortlessly handles the fleece bulk and the corresponding larger handle is comfortable to use, making it easier on my hands.

Choose the 45mm rotary decorative blades (wave, pinking or scallop) for specialty edge finishes.

Olfa offers a variety of specialty blades. The wave blade gives a soft, gentle fleece edge. The pinking blade finish lends a crafty flavor. The Olfa scallop blade offers two decorative edges: scallops on one cut edge and peaks on the opposite edge.

Choose the 45mm rotary decorative blades (wave, pinking or scallop) for specialty edge finishes.

Olfa offers a variety of specialty blades. The wave blade gives a soft, gentle fleece edge. The pinking blade finish lends a crafty flavor. The Olfa scallop blade offers two decorative edges: scallops on one cut edge and peaks on the opposite edge.

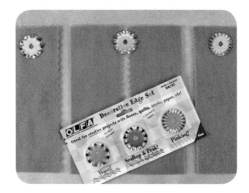

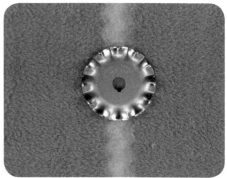

nancy's note

There are many decorative blade scissors on the market that are designed for use on paper and perhaps flat cotton. They do not work well on fleece.

Depending on how you attach the blade and/or cut the fabric, you can have either a scallop or peaked edge. Cutting in the usual way, with the Olfa logo on the blade facing the handle, you will have a scalloped edge. If you have the logo facing away from the handle, you will have a peaked edge. (Always do a sample test cut when using the scallop blade to make sure you get the edge shape you want.)

Olfa Chenille Cutter

This new sewing tool makes slashing the channels for chenille a quick and easy process.

After stitching the parallel diagonal rows, simply turn the ratchet dial counterclockwise to choose the best channel guide (foot) that "fits your channel" and then easily slice the top layer. When making fleece chenille, your channels will be ⅜" wide, so choose the LL channel guide. But always test first to see which guide fills the channel the best.

nancy's note

Have a pair of serger tweezers handy. Fleece lint builds up quickly on the cutter blade. Tweeze and remove lint, as it interferes with slashing.

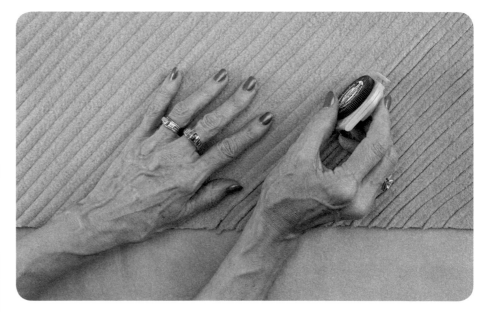

The blade is a special blade, finely honed, extra sharp and designed for slicing fabric. (Since the blade is stationary and does not rotate, the blade needs to be sharper than a traditional rotary blade.)

When the blade becomes dull, simply turn the ratchet-dial clockwise to expose a new section of the blade. You have 24 different cutting edges to use before needing to replace the blade!

Omnigrid Mini Omnistrips

These are long, skinny, strips of cutting mats. They are designed for the precision cutting of chenille channels.

The Omnistrips come in a variety of widths from ¼" to ⅝". They are packaged in two ways: Omni Strips (⅜", ½" and ⅝" strip widths) and Mini Omnistrips (¼", ⁵⁄₁₆" and ⅜" widths). I use the Mini Omnistrip group the most, but if you make both fleece and woven/cotton chenille, you will want the strip widths offered in both packages.

Appliqué Scissors

With its flat, disc-shaped, underside blade, appliqué scissors provide close, accurate trimming while protecting the remaining under-layers of fabric from unintentional nicks and cuts. They are the best way to achieve a clean blunt-edge trim on all appliqués.

Rounded-Tip Trimming Scissors by Heritage Cutlery

I love my appliqué scissors and use them a lot. However, I found that in close trimming of fleece, the sharp points of the appliqué scissors frequently catch on, and sometimes snag, the fleece surface.

I explained this "snag" concern to Heritage Cutlery, who then came up with the perfect answer—round-tipped appliqué scissors (with cushioned handles as a bonus!).

I fell in love with them for trimming fleece (appliqués, fat piping finish, appliqué edges, etc.), but also found they are wonderful for trimming stabilizer from embroidered terry cloth (no more catching the scissor points in the terry loops) and heirloom trimming (protects delicate laces).

These scissors do not replace the traditional sharp-pointed scissors; they are an "added" pair. (I still need the sharp points for precision cutting in corners and tight spaces.)

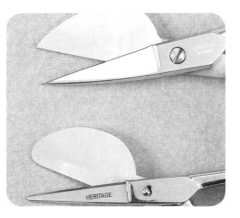

Heritage Cutlery's Rounded-Tip Trimming Scissors solve the problem of snagging fleece with the points of other scissors tips.

June Tailor Fancy Fleece Ruler

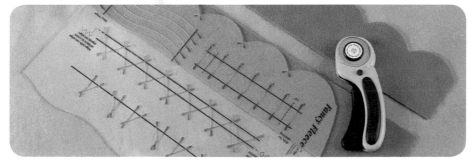

This terrific ruler makes it easy to cut dramatic, shaped edges on fleece. Designed for use with a standard 45mm straight blade rotary cutter, choose from wavy, scallop or zigzag cut edges; wavy fringe; triangular or diamond-shaped cutouts; or spaced slits for weaving accent trim. (Don't forget about this ruler for craft and school projects.)

fleece techniques

Quick Fringe

I have featured this technique in all my books. It is easy and quick. Use the grid markings on the cutting mats to measure fringe width and depth, which is so much easier than constantly sliding a ruler or inserting a blade into a slot.

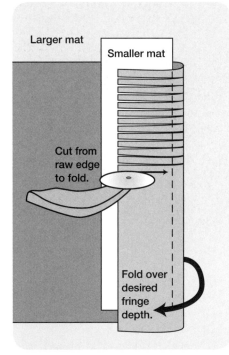

Larger mat

Smaller mat

Cut from raw edge to fold.

Fold over desired fringe depth.

nancy's note to quilters

When cutting and sewing quilt blocks, precision is critical. When cutting fleece fringe, "close counts." Set aside your ruler and enjoy the easy nature of fleece.

Directions

1. Lay the fleece edge that is to be fringed on top of a large cutting mat.

2. Lay a smaller cutting mat on top of the fleece, sandwiching the fleece between the two mats. Position the smaller mat so the edge to be fringed extends beyond the small mat edge.

3. Fold the fleece to be fringed back onto the smaller cutting mat, using the grid lines to judge the depth of the fringe and alignment of the cuts. Keep the fleece taut against the small mat edge.

4. Begin at the raw edge of the fleece on the smaller mat and rotary cut the fringe by running the cutter onto the larger mat.

Quick Fringe Basics

- Fringe-cuts can be virtually any width. The most common and most effective are fringe-cuts between ½" and 1" wide.
- Unless you have a specific design need, never cut fringe narrower than ½" when the fringe is cut on the crossgrain (fringe-cuts perpendicular to the selvage). Fringe-cuts on the crossgrain are stretchy. Narrow, stretchy fringe-cuts distort easily.
- Never cut fringe narrower than ½" on baby or toddler items. Narrower fringe can potentially break off and present a swallowing danger.
- Fringe-cuts can be virtually any length. The most common—and most effective—are between 2-½" and 5" long.
- Quick fringe-cuts can be made using a straight or specialty blade rotary cutter.
- The width and length of the fringe and the choice of blade edge are governed by the end use, the fleece print and personal taste. There is no right or wrong choice.

Blunt-Edge Appliqué

The Soccer Pillow, page 58, features Blunt-Edge Appliqué using the Cut-and-Stitch Method. Precutting the appliqués allows you to arrange and rearrange motifs until you have a look and balance you like.

Appliqué is a popular embellishment in all areas of sewing. It is especially popular with fleece because it is so easy to do, and this particular technique for appliqué is truly the no-hassle method!

I could have named this technique Raw-Edge Appliqué, but "blunt-edge" is more descriptive. The cut edge of fleece is clean and blunt, and because fleece doesn't ravel, it stays that way.

The Blunt-Edge Appliqué technique applies to the appliqué itself. The appliqué fabric is fleece. It is not necessary to satin stitch finish the raw edges! (You could if you wanted to, but you don't have to. It looks so good and is so quick to make as-is, why do the extra work?)

The appliqué can be placed onto any base fabric. Fleece appliqué on fleece, on denim, on cotton, on corduroy, on muslin, etc. You get the idea.

The appliqué can be made from print fleece (using the printed design) or from solid fleece (with your own design traced onto the fabric).

There are two ways to approach making the appliqué: Cut-and-Stitch Method or its opposite, the Stitch-and-Cut Method. There is no hard-and-fast rule as to which one to choose. The appliqué motif shape will dictate which method makes most sense.

Cut-and-Stitch Method

The appliqué on both of these Winter Scene Pillows, page 112, was applied using the Cut-and-Stitch Method. See the explanation that follows as to why this method works best in this situation.

The Cut-and-Stitch Method is best used when the design has simple outer edges and/or when exact placement is critical. Cut out the motif first and then edgestitch it in place.

Here's how:

1. Cut out the fleece motif.

2. Lightly spray the wrong side of the cutout with temporary spray adhesive.

3. Adhere the cutout fleece appliqué in place.

4. Edgestitch appliqué in place. Use an edgestitching, edge guide or edge joining presser foot and move your needle to either left or right needle position for easy and accurate stitch placement.

Why use the Cut-and-Stitch Method in this situation?

The simple geometric motifs are easy to cut, place precisely and edgestitch in place. The shapes are linear; there are no nooks and crannies that might present a challenge to keep the edgestitching consistent. .Also, the exact placement of the appliqué is critical, so cutting the motifs out first and then stitching them in place (cut and stitch) is the proper technique choice because it is the easiest.

Stitch-and-Cut Method

The Jaguar Pillow, page 116, features the Stitch-and-Cut Method because the busier appliqué edges made them difficult to edgestitch accurately.

The Stitch-and-Cut Method is used when the appliqué has busier edges, making it more challenging to edgestitch them accurately. Stitch the motif in place first and then trim excess fleece from the motif's stitched edges.

Here's how:

1. Cut out a patch of print fleece, leaving a "rough border" all around the motif.

2. Lay the appliqué patch on the base fabric and stitch on the outer edge of the desired motif.

3. Use appliqué scissors to trim excess fleece close to the stitching line.

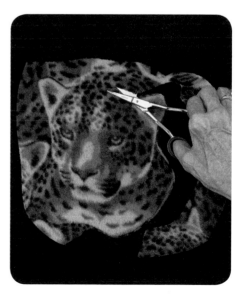

Why use the Stitch-and-Cut Method in this situation?

As you can see, the jaguar face appliqué was not as easy to accurately edgestitch as the trees and soccer ball in the Cut-and-Stitch Method examples. And, the irregular shape of the jaguar face makes it easy to "center" the motif on the pillow front. So here, the Cut-and-Stitch Method is easier method to use.

Blunt-Edge Appliqué with Solids

The Easy Appliquéd Cape, page 86, features solid-colored fleece appliqué applied using the Blunt-Edge Appliqué technique.

When using solid-colored fleece for your appliqué, first trace the appliqué design onto the right side of the fleece and then use either the Cut-and-Stitch or Stitch-and-Cut methods of the Blunt-Edge Appliqué technique.

nancy's
note to embroidery machine owners

You can easily take advantage of your embroidery design library and do the Stitch-and-Cut Method of Blunt-Edge Appliqué on your embroidery machine. Refer to Embroidery Machine Essentials: Fleece Techniques for more information.

Either the Cut-and-Stitch or Stitch-and-Cut methods works when your appliqué is made from a solid-colored fleece. The only difference is that you first need to trace the appliqué design onto the right side of the solid fleece piece. Refer to page 11 for how to use Clover Mesh Transfer Canvas and water-soluble pencils to draw the design.

Double-Sided Blunt-Edge Appliqué

This variation of the Stitch-and-Cut Method for Blunt-Edge Appliqué results in having appliqués on both sides of the base fabric. The back-to-back appliqués look tedious to make but are deceptively easy. It is perfect for blankets and scarves.

This Patriotic Scarf, page 104, has star appliqués on both sides of the scarf that were appliquéd simultaneously.

Directions

Since each appliqué is really two appliqués (one on each side of the base fabric), you will need two appliqué pieces of fleece for each appliqué.

1. Cut two fleece appliqué pieces for each appliqué. Cut pieces 2" larger all around than the size of the finished appliqué.

2. Use Clover Mesh Transfer Canvas and water-soluble pencils to trace the appliqué motif on the right side of one fleece appliqué piece.

3. Pin the *traced* appliqué piece, with *right* sides facing up, on top of the main fleece project (scarf, blanket, vest, etc.)

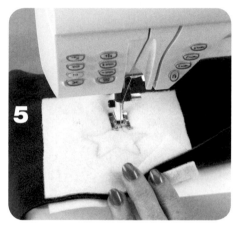

4. Pin the *untraced* appliqué piece, with *wrong* sides together, on the backside of the main fleece project, sandwiching the project between the appliqué pieces. (This is why the appliqué pieces are cut larger than needed. The alignment does not need to be exact.)

5. Stitch the motif, sewing through the traced appliqué piece, the project fabric and the under-layer appliqué piece.

6. Use appliqué scissors to trim the excess fleece from the outer edges of the stitching on both appliqué pieces, trimming close to the stitching line.

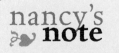

nancy's note

I pin rather than use spray adhesive to hold the appliqué pieces in place because if any of the adhesive is outside the appliqué perimeter, it would interfere with the trimming process.

Reverse Appliqué

The Jaguar Blanket, page 116, show how beautifully the finished piece turns out when using the Reverse Appliqué technique.

Reverse appliqué with fleece is similar to traditional reverse appliqué, except that it is much easier—just like everything else with fleece! When using fleece, you don't have to finish the edges.

As in traditional reverse appliqué, you need two layers of fabric (a double-layer blanket, scarf or vest). You can combine a print fleece with a solid fleece or choose two solid fleeces.

Print-and-Solid Reverse Appliqué

The print-and-solid combination is easy because the fleece print provides you with the appliqué motifs. Choose a print with a relatively well-defined motif to outline stitch (soccer ball, leaf, simple flower, animal, heart, etc.). You will be trimming that shape, so you don't want difficult nooks and crannies. For example, you wouldn't want to trim moose antlers! Besides being difficult to trim, fussy detail is lost on fleece.

Here's how:

1. Place the fleece layers with *wrong* sides together (finished position).

2. Determine which print motifs to highlight. (In the finished project, the print won't look much different on the printed fleece side, but will be visible on the solid side of the blanket, scarf, vest, etc.).

3. Stitch around the motifs, using a 3mm straight stitch.

4. Use appliqué scissors to trim away the *solid layer only* from within the stitched motif, working from the solid fleece side. Trim close to the stitching line.

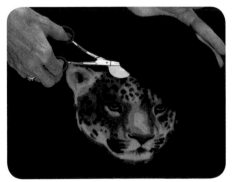

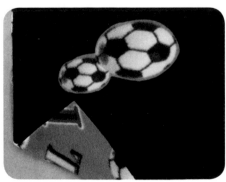

nancy's notes

Choosing Motifs
If you are using an allover print with several motifs, it can be hard to decide what motifs to stitch around. I like to lay my pinned-together, double-layer project on the floor, print side up, and place pieces of paper on the motifs I intend to stitch and trim. I move the papers around until I get a balanced look, then pin the papers in place so I know where to sew.

Choosing Where to Trim
When you trim away the solid fleece layer in the stitched outline, a bit of fleece will remain. You need to decide whether the outline stitching should be exactly on the motif edge or outside of it. There is no right or wrong choice. If you sew on the outline, the remaining fleece will crowd the motif on the trimmed side. If you align the outer edge of your presser foot alongside the motif's outer edge, the stitching will be about ¼" away from the motif edge; once the solid side is trimmed, the color around the motif will act as a border.

Solid-and-Solid Reverse Appliqué

The Heart Blanket and Coordinating Heart Pillow, page 64, are examples of how solid fleece can be used with the Reverse Appliqué technique.

Creating Reverse Appliqué motifs with two solid layers of fleece requires transfer of an appliqué design onto the fleece first.

Here's how:

1. Use Clover Mesh Transfer Canvas and water-soluble pencils to trace your desired appliqué motifs onto the right side of one of the fleece solid layers.

2. Place fleece layers wrong sides together (finished position).

3. Outline stitch motifs using a 3mm straight stitch.

4. Use appliqué scissors to trim away the solid layer only from within the stitched motif. Trim close to the stitching line.

Fleece Chenille

Use the Fleece Chenille technique to create beautiful designs like that featured on the Jaguar Chenille Pillow, page 116.

The Fleece Chenille technique is similar to the traditional Faux Chenille® technique developed by Nanette Holmberg. However, creating fleece chenille is much easier and faster to make. You only need two layers of fabric—not the traditional six layers! And it blooms the instant you slash open the top layer, so there's no roughing and brushing, no straggly threads and no tossing in the washer and dryer required to get it to "bloom."

Fleece Chenille Basics

High contrast between layers of fleece results in a more dramatic and noticeable chenille effect.

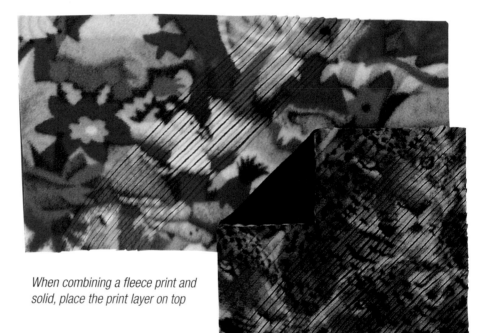

When combining a fleece print and solid, place the print layer on top

- Select high-quality mid-weight fleece.
- The stronger the color contrast between the two fleece layers, the more noticeable and dramatic the chenille effect.
- If the two fleece layers are similar in color tone, the end result is a more tonal textured effect.
- Combining a fleece print with a coordinating solid dramatizes the print with texture. Place the print layer on top.
- The rows of channel stitching must be sewn on the bias.
- There is no hard-and-fast rule as to whether the diagonal lines should run from upper left to lower right or the opposite. If a print is complemented by the stitching lines running one angle vs. the other, by all means complement the print.
- For best results, space parallel channels ⅜" apart. (¼" rows are too narrow to slash open; ⅜" spacing results in a plush look, while ½" spacing is OK and ⅝" or wider channels look chunky.)
- Make chenille yardage first and then cut out individual pattern pieces from that yardage.

Chenille Yardage

In most instances, you will make chenille yardage first and then cut out the individual pattern pieces. When handling two layers of fleece and sewing row upon row of parallel bias stitching lines, shifting of the fabric layers is unavoidable. Therefore, begin with larger pieces than you really need so you can disregard the uneven edges and still have enough chenille yardage to cut out your pattern pieces.

Here's How:

1. Layer larger-than-needed pieces of fleece with either wrong sides together, right sides facing out if the unslashed side of chenille will be visible in the finished project (like a double layer vest) or with both right sides facing up if unslashed side will not be visible (like a pillow top).

    a. Allocate a *minimum* of 2" larger all around (on smaller projects) or 4" larger all around (on larger projects).

2. Sew parallel rows of stitching on the bias, spaced ⅜" apart. Adjust stitch length to 3mm to 3.5mm. Keep the rows as straight and parallel as possible.

    a. Using a water-soluble pencil, draw a line on the fleece at a 45-degree angle to the straight or cross grain. If combining a print and a solid, draw line on the solid for best visibility.

    b. Draw additional lines 3" apart and parallel to the first bias line.

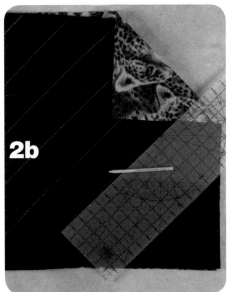

    c. Use the lines as a helpful guide for keeping stitching lines straight. If you find your stitching lines getting off-kilter, gradually alter the stitching lines to get back to the correct angle. Don't worry about uneven or messy beginnings and endings of the stitching channels or uneven fabric edges. That's why you began with a larger-than-needed piece.

nancy's note

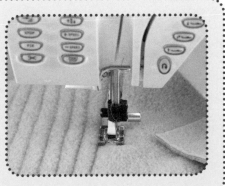

If you are having a difficult time spacing your ⅜" stitching lines consistently, try moving your needle to the far right needle position and align the left edge of the presser foot along the preciously sewn stitching line.

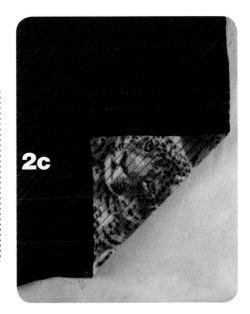

3. Slash open the top layer only of each channel, cutting down the middle of the channel using one of the following methods.

3a

a. Use Omnigrid Mini Omnistrips for an easy way to slash the upper layer on straight rows by inserting a Mini Omnistrip between layers and then cutting with a rotary cutter. The mini cutting mat protects the bottom layer from being cut. Sew the channel ⅛" wider than the width of the mini cutting strip you will use. Space the stitching lines ⅜" apart when using the ¼" mini strips and ½" apart when using the ⅜" mini strip.

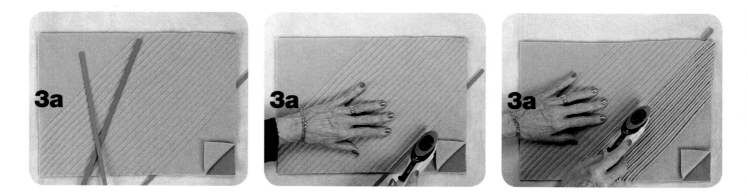

3a 3a 3a

b. The Olfa Chenille Cutter offers four channel guide widths in one handy little tool. (Refer to page 12 for specifics.) Choose the large channel guide for fleece chenille. Insert the guide between the layers and easily slice open the top fleece layer. If you have difficulty beginning the slash cut, make a small snip with scissors to help you get started. If the cutter gets dull, turn the dial one "click" to expose a new cutting section on the blade.

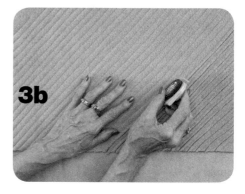

3b

nancy's note

If you are slashing chenille yardage, use the Chenille Cutter or the Mini Omnistrips for clean, consistent slash cuts. On small projects involving "unsecured edges" (like a cutout chenille appliqué where there are no locking stitches at the cut edges of the motif), I prefer to use the round-tipped trimming scissors to cut open the top layer. If my project size is medium to larger is size and has "unsecured edges," use the Chenille cutter or ministrips. If you use the Chenille Cutter, use scissors to make a small starter cut to alleviate strain on the unsecured stitches.

Chenille Appliqué

The Chenille Leaf Throw, page 122, was completed by using the Chenille Appliqué technique.

Materials Needed

Fleece for appliqués (large enough for a double layer for each appliqué)
Clover Mesh Transfer Canvas
Water-soluble pencil
Appliqué scissors
Olfa Mini Omnistrips
Pins or temporary spray adhesive
Tape measure

Chenille Appliqué is a mini-version of the Fleece Chenille technique. You make a small piece of chenille yardage, cut out the appliqué shape, slash the channels and edgestitch in place.

The appliqué can be used as an embellishment on any fabric type (fleece, denim, muslin, quilt fabrics, etc.)

Here's how:

1. Follow the directions for Chenille Yardage, page 123, and sew parallel bias rows of stitching on a double layer of fleece large enough to very generously accommodate the number of appliqués needed. Place both layers of fleece with right sides facing up. Do not slash open the channels yet.

2. Use Clover Mesh Transfer Canvas and a water-soluble pencil to trace the appliqué motifs onto the chenille yardage. (You can draw the motifs at any angle or direction to make the chenille cuts flatter the appliqué design. Since it is the stitched rows that need to be on the bias, and they already are, you can arrange the appliqué shape as desired.)

3. Cut out the traced (still unslashed) yardage into drawn appliqué shapes.

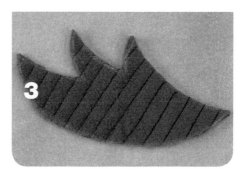

4. Slash open the top layer only of each channel.

> **a.** Be careful when cutting these channels open. Remember that there are no locked stitches at the cut edges.

> **b.** Use appliqué scissors to cut the top layer. I especially like the round-tipped trimming scissors for this step. If your appliqué is large, use the Mini Omnistrips.

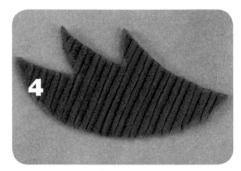

5. Arrange the appliqué(s) on the project as desired. Pin or lightly spray the wrong side of chenille appliqué with temporary adhesive spray and adhere.

6. Edgestitch the appliqué to the base fabric.

> **a.** Place the presser foot so it is completely on the appliqué and its right outer edge is aligned to the outer edge of the appliqué.

> **b.** Move the needle position to the right (for a skimpy ¼" topstitching line).

> **c.** Use a stiletto (or seam ripper, small screwdriver, wooden cuticle stick) as necessary to encourage the chenille cuts to lay flat for topstitching.

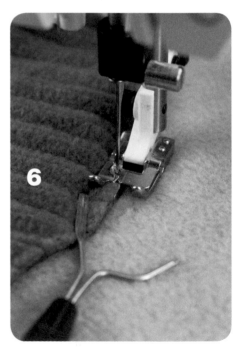

7. Use appliqué scissors, as necessary, to trim and neaten the outer edges of appliqué.

Chenille Strips

The Blooming Blanket project, page 66, makes use of the Chenille Strips technique.

This is my fleece version of Fabric Café's™ clever Chenille-by-the-Inch™. Chenille strips are easy to make and offer a great texture that can be used for embellishment on jackets, quilts, in landscape scenes, with appliqués, and of course, on fleece.

Here's how:

1. Use a pinking blade rotary cutter to cut two ½" x 60" strips of fleece on the crossgrain (with the greater stretch going in the length.)

2. Lay one pinked strip on top of the other with *both wrong sides* facing up. (To find the wrong side, refer to page 8.)

3. Stitch the layers together, using a stretch stitch or narrow zigzag (2mm wide x 2.5mm long) and sewing down the center of the strips.

4. Stretch the fleece firmly, drawing it through your pinched fingers. The fleece will curl up on itself and form a long chenille strip. (That's why the strips were placed with both wrong sides facing up.)

5. Place wash-away basting tape on the back (flat) side of the chenille strip.

6. Adhere the strip where desired on the project.

7. Stitch the strip in place by sewing down the middle using a 4mm long straight stitch.

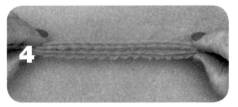

nancy's note

For an easy way to keep the strips together and your stitching centered, place your index fingers alongside both sides of the presser foot to form a tunnel and feed the strips under the presser foot.

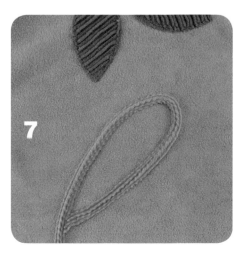

Reverse Hem

The Heart Blanket, page 64, is finished using a Reverse Hem binding.

The Reverse Hem technique is a no-hassle way to bind a blanket edge by "framing" it. Because fleece doesn't ravel, we can do a "cheater's mitered corner," which is quick and easy.

Overview: The back layer of the blanket is fleece, cut larger than the face of the blanket, and folded from back-to-front, enclosing the blanket face's raw edges. The blanket back *must* be fleece (for this technique), but the blanket face can be any fabric (fleece, flannel, cotton, novelty knit, etc.). When choosing a blanket front fabric that shrinks with laundering (like cotton flannel), make sure to pre-launder that fabric before sewing. Fleece does not need to be pre-laundered.

Directions

Note: In these directions, the finished frame is 2".

1. Cut the blanket front the desired size.

2. Cut the blanket back two times the "frame depth" larger than the blanket front. The blanket back may be cut with a straight or decorative rotary blade. Example: the blanket front is 45" square.

> **a.** For a 1" frame, cut fleece blanket back 47" square (2 x 1" frame = 2", so 2" + 45" front = 47" back).
>
> **b.** For a 2" frame, cut fleece blanket back 49" square (2 x 2" frame = 4", so 4" + 45" front = 49").
>
> **c.** For a 3" frame, cut blanket back 51" square (2 x 3" frame = 6", so 6" + 45" front = 51").

3. Lay the fleece back on a table, *wrong* side facing up. (To find the right side of fleece, refer to page 8.) Center the blanket front, *right* side facing up, on top of the fleece blanket back, leaving a 2" fleece back border extending beyond all the blanket front edges. If necessary, trim the fleece edges so you have an even border.

4. Fold a 2" fleece hem along the top edge of the blanket, encasing the blanket front raw edge. Pin the hem in place. Beginning and ending at the *blanket front edges*, edgestitch the fleece hem.

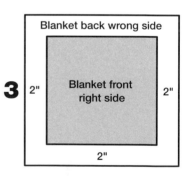

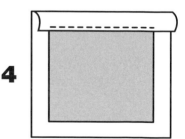

5

5. Trim the upper right corner of the blanket back *hem only.*

6. Fold and pin a 2" fleece hem along the right edge of the blanket, encasing the blanket front raw edge. Stitch from the inner corner to the outer corner (cheater's mitered corner).

7. Trim the excess fleece corner wedge piece.

8. Edgestitch the fleece side hem, stopping at the edge of the blanket front.

9. Repeat Steps 4 through 8 to miter the remaining three corners and edgestitch the hems.

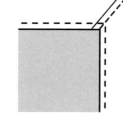

6

7

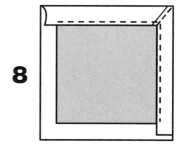

8

9

This blanket features a reverse hem encasing the raw edges of the flannel blanket front. The flannel was pre-laundered before sewing to remove shrinkage. The fleece layer was cut with a decorative-edge rotary blade.

Cheater's Wrapped Edge (a.k.a. Fat Piping)

Both the Dog Lover's Vest, page 81, and the Chenille-Yoked Vest, page 78, are finished with the Cheater's Wrapped Edge technique.

This clever edge finish mimics piping and is a great technique to remember for edge finishing everything from hats to blankets, sleeve hems, baby wraps, towels and more. It is suitable as an edge finish on any raw edge for any project (quilted vest, flannel blanket, etc.). It is an easy, nonbulky edge finish you will use over and over again.

The only qualification is that the trim used for the edge finish *must* be a knit because a knit has stretch and it doesn't ravel. Throughout this book, fleece is used for the trim, but you could substitute ribbing, Lycra, stretch velour, knit terry, interlock or any other knit. When choosing to use a trim fabric other than fleece, make sure it is washable and colorfast. When choosing fleece as your trim, there are no washability or colorfast concerns.

Directions

Since fleece is used as the trim throughout this book, the directions are written specifically for fleece trim. (Refer to *More Polar Magic* for in-depth Cheater's Wrapped Edge information, alternative fabric choices, end uses, tips and tricks, recommended widths for various projects and more.)

1. Determine the desired finished trim width. (This information will be given in the directions for specific projects throughout the book.)

2. Cut the fleece trim strip on the crossgrain (from selvage to selvage, with the greater degree of stretch). Cut fleece trim a *minimum* of four times the seam allowance width. If you have enough fleece, five or six times the seam allowance width is even easier to handle.

3. Pin a single layer of fleece trim strip, with right sides together, to the project cut edge. Keep the raw edges even.

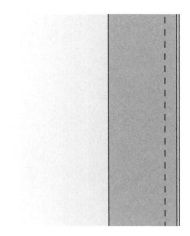

4. Place the project against the machine feed teeth of a conventional sewing machine with the trim strip on top. Do not use a serger for this step. You do not want to trim away any seam allowance.

5. Stitch precisely, using the project directions' specified seam allowance width. (You will be wrapping this seam allowance with the trim. Any uneven stitching will be obvious.) Do not cut away any fabric or trim.

6. Wrap the fleece trim strip to the wrong side of the project. Pin it in place.

    a. Wrap the strip up, over and around the raw edges, encasing the trim and the project raw edges.

    b. Working from the right side of the project, pin the strip in the finished position. Make sure the trim is uniform. (The excess trim will generously overlap the stitching line on the wrong side.)

7. Use an edgestitch or edge-joining presser foot for precise stitch placement and stitch-in-the-ditch on the right side of the project to secure the wrapped trim strip to the backside. (Stitch-in-the-ditch means to stitch on the previously sewn seamline.)

8. Use appliqué scissors to cut the excess trim close to the stitching line on the backside of the project.

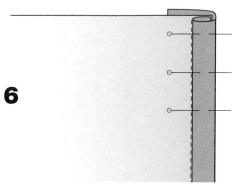

splicing trim

Whether you use precut Lycra trim strips or make your own strips from fleece or other knit fabrics, there will be times when you need to join strips to have enough trim length to complete the project.

Here's how:

1. Place the trim strips, with right sides together, at a 45-degree angle and stitch a bias seam.

2. Trim the seam allowance to ¼".

3. Finger-press the seam open.

4. Continue splicing strips until you have the length you need.

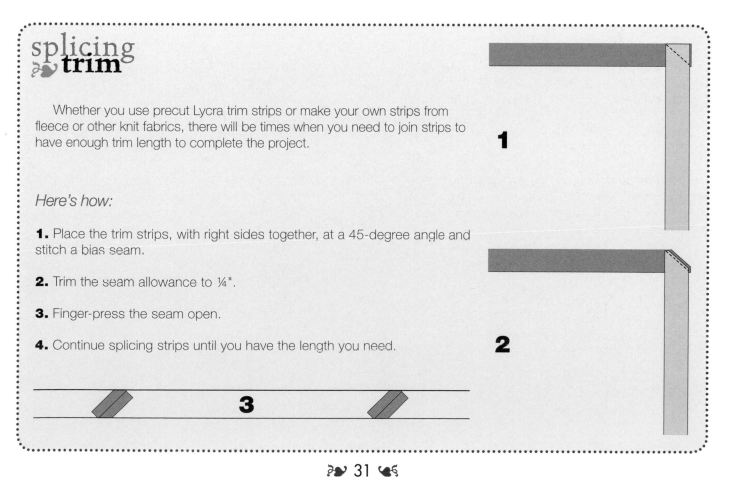

Cheater's Wrapped Edge Hints, Tips and Cautions

You need to be more careful when wrapping the edge of a single-layer project (a single-layer blanket or a single-layer vest) than a double-layered item. By the time you have finished wrapping the edge, you will have three layers of trim encasing the single-layer edge of your project. It is important to "handle" the trim "appropriately" to avoid overpowering the single layer. Double-layered items have a bit more weight involved, so they are less affected by three layers in the wrap.

Single-Layer Blanket

Goal: Long side edges that don't draw up and corners that don't buckle under.

1. Trim the blanket corners into a gentle, rounded corner.

2. Lengthen the stitch to 3.5mm.

3. Sew the trim to the blanket with a one-to-one ratio on the long, straight sides of blanket. Do not stretch either layer when sewing. Gently guide the trim, but do not stretch it.

4. Sew slower and "force-feed" the trim a little bit into the curve on the curved corners. In other words, try to ease in a little more trim length than blanket length.

Single-Layer Vest

Goal: Center front and hems that lay flat, center front corner that doesn't buckle under, and armholes and back neck edge that don't gap or curl outward.

1. Cut the lower edge of the vest center front into a rounded point/curve.

2. Lengthen the stitch to 3.5mm.

3. Sew the trim to the vest with a one-to-one ratio on the long straight edges (center front, V-neck and lower edge). Do not stretch either layer. Gently guide the trim, but do not stretch it.

4. Sew slower and "force-feed" the trim a little bit into the curve on the center front lower-edge curved point. In other words, try to ease in a little more trim length than vest length.

5. Stretch the trim moderately in the lower third of the armhole only when sewing it to the vest. For the upper two-thirds of the armhole, sew with a one-to-one ratio.

6. Stretch the trim slightly to moderately only when sewing the trim to the back neck edge between the shoulder seams.

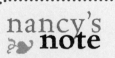

nancy's
note

The stretching of the trim at the inside curved areas of the lower armhole and at the back neck edge causes the garment to cup in and hug the body, rather than gap outward.

Pillow Construction and Fat Piping Edge Finish

Pillows of varying sizes and styles are featured throughout the book. They are easily finished in 90 minutes and accent the décor in any room.

The pillows in this book are simple, envelope-style pillows that make room décor changeovers quick and easy.

The following Materials Needed and Directions are given for a plain pillow using a 16" pillow form. Add yardage as necessary for chosen embellishments. Information for 14", 18" and 20" pillows can be found on page 35.

Appliqués and Pillow Size

The appliqué motifs will frequently dictate the pillow size to choose. Allow a minimum of 1½" space between the edge of an appliqué and the fat piping seam. Most appliqués will look better with more surrounding space. Each print is different.

Directions

1. Cut one 4" x 60" trim strip from the contrast fleece color for the fat piping edge finish.

2. Cut one 19" square pillow front (3" larger than the pillow form) and two 17½" x 12¾" pillow half-backs from the main fleece color.

    a. If you have enough fleece and nap or print is not an issue, cut the 17½" in the direction of the least stretch. Since you are making an envelope-style closing on the backside of the pillow, the overlap lays nicer if the stretch is cut in this direction.

    b. Starting with a 19" square pillow front, then trimming to 17½" square provides a fudge factor in case appliqués are not centered exactly or something shifts during the embellishing process. If you are not embellishing the pillow front, or are short on yardage, you may cut pillow fronts to 17½" square.

3. Embellish the pillow front as desired by first arranging and temporarily affixing appliqué pieces and then stitching them in place.

4. Retrue and trim the pillow front to 17½" square (1½" larger than the pillow form).

5. Turn under and topstitch 2" hems on one long edge of each half-back.

Materials Needed for 16" pillow

Fleece main color solid (for pillow): ⅝ yard mid-weight fleece
Fleece contrast color (for fat piping): ⅛ yard
Fleece appliqué or embellishment: as needed
16" square pillow form
Thread to match main fleece drop (needle)
Thread to match contrast fleece drop (bobbin)
100/16 universal needle* drop (for construction)
Appliqué scissors (pointed or round-tipped)
Use a larger needle size to accommodate the added bulk of the fat piping.

(diagram: rectangle labeled 17-½" across top, 5 at left, 2" at bottom left)

6. Overlap the half-back hems 4" and baste them together using a ¾" seam allowance.

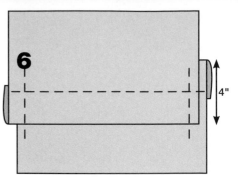

7. Pin the pillow front to the basted pillow half-backs with *wrong* sides together (finished position).

8. Place the right side of the 4" trim strip (from Step 1) against the right side of the pillow front.

9. Use an *exact* ¾" seam allowance and begin sewing 5" from the end of the trim strip. (You are sewing through three layers: trim strip, pillow front and pillow back.) To avoid additional bulk when splicing the strip ends, do not begin this stitching in the pillow back overlap area.

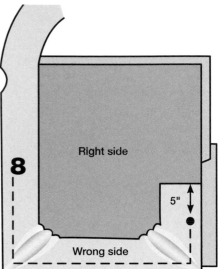

Right side

Wrong side

nancy's ⁊ note

It is important to stretch the trim moderately as you stitch it to the pillow front. It gives a taut finish. Also, if you don't stretch, you will not have the needed trim length.

10. Sew the trim strip to the outer edge of the pillow. Moderately stretch the trim strip while sewing. Pivot at the corners. Stop sewing exactly 5" before the beginning stitching.

11. Cut the ending edge of the strip exactly 4" beyond the ending stitching.

12. Lift up both unsewn ends of the trim strip. Match and pin edges, as illustrated, with right sides together. (Pin first, check and then proceed. It's easier to unpin than it is to tear out stitching!)

13. Sew A to B "on the diagonal," beginning exactly at the corner of B.

14. Double-check the right side of the spliced strip before trimming to make sure everything looks correct. If satisfied, trim the seam allowance to ¼" and finger-press seam allowance open.

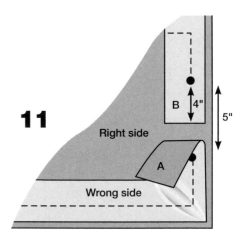

Right side

Wrong side

15. Finish sewing the last 5" of the spliced trim strip to the pillow.

16. Trim away one seam allowance layer in the overlap area—only on the half-backs—to make the bulk comparable to the rest of the pillow. Don't trim away any other seam allowance. In the following steps, when wrapping and enclosing the seam allowance, the fluffiness of the fleece "plumps" the wrap and gives a fat piping appearance.

17. Wrap the trim strip to the backside, wrapping up, over and around to encase the raw edge of the seam allowances. Trim just the tips of the pillow corners for ease in wrapping.

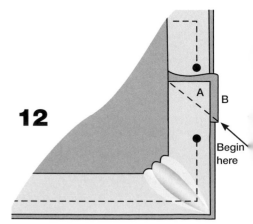

Begin here

18. Work from the front of the pillow and pin the trim strip in place. Make sure the plump, wrapped edges are uniform. Manipulate the trim around the corners, as necessary, so it rounds the corners and lays flat on the pillow back.

19. Use an edgestitch or edge-joining presser foot for precise stitch placement and stitch-in-the-ditch on the right side of the pillow to secure the wrapped trim strip. (Stitch-in-the-ditch means to stitch on the previously sewn seamline.) Use needle thread that matches the main fleece color (pillow) and bobbin thread that matches the contrast color (fat piping).

20. Use appliqué scissors to cut the excess trim close to the stitching line on the back of the pillow.

21. Insert the pillow form through the flap opening.

Finishing Tip: Pillow forms come in a variety of quantities and plumpness. If your pillow form does not fill the pillow corners fully, insert some polyester stuffing.

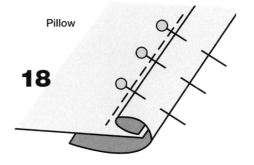

Pillow

18

nancy's note

One 4" x 60" strip will make fat piping for a 14" or 16" pillow form. Two 4" x 60" strips, spliced together, are needed for a pillow form 18" or larger. (Refer to Splicing Trim directions on page 31.)

Information for Different Pillow Sizes

20" Pillow Form
Main yardage: ⅔ yard
Contrast yardage: ¼ yard (for fat piping)

1. Cut two 4" x 60" contrast strips (for fat piping).

2. Splice trim strips to make one long trim strip. (Refer to Splicing Trim directions on page 31.)

3. Cut the pillow front 23" square (3" larger than pillow form).

4. Cut two 21½" x 14¾" half-backs.

5. Trim the pillow front to 21½" square.

18" Pillow Form
Main yardage: ⅝ yard
Contrast yardage: ¼ yard (for fat piping)

1. Cut two 4" x 60" contrast strips (for fat piping).

2. Splice trim strips to make one long trim strip. (Refer to Splicing Trim directions on page 31.)

3. Cut the pillow front 21" square (3" larger than pillow form)

4. Cut two 19½" x 13¾" half-backs.

5. Trim the pillow front to 19½" square.

14" Pillow Form
Main yardage: ½ yard
Contrast yardage: ⅛ yard (for fat piping)

1. Cut one 4" x 60" contrast strip (for fat piping).

2. Cut the pillow front 17" square (3" larger than pillow form).

3. Cut two 15½" x 11¾" half-backs.

4. Trim the pillow front to 15½" square.

Multisized Vest Pattern and General Sewing Information

This moderately-sized vest is easy to construct. Although it can be sewn in a number of the "traditional" ways, this book details a variety of easy fleece finishes.

Use this simple vest as a "canvas," a starting point for creating a variety of finished looks.

The vest can be:

- Single- or double-layer
- Decorative or plain, exposed seam allowances
- Finished with Cheater's Wrapped Edge
- Embellished with chenille or appliqués
- With a stand-up square or round collar
- V-neck or jewel neck (neckline without the collar)
- Straight hem or shirttail hem

So, although the vest is simple, it offers a wide range of possibilities.

Pattern Tracing Material

To preserve the master multisized pattern for future use, I highly recommend that you use a pattern tracing material and trace the vest you are going to make. Trace your pattern with a soft-lead pencil. (That way, if any marking happens to transfer onto your fabric, it will easily wash out.)

Using a Multisized Pattern

The beauty of working with a multisized pattern is that most of us are "multisized." Choose the vest size according to your bust measurement and size in or out, as necessary, for the hip area.

Example: If your bust measures one size (let's say medium) and your hips measure a different size (let's be realistic here and say large), then trace the medium vest neck, shoulders and armhole. As you draw down the side seam, grade the pattern out to the large size in the hip area. (You should be on the medium line at the bust, halfway to the large in the waist area and all the way to the large line in the hip area.)

If you are tall or short, or just want a longer or shorter vest, make the length adjustments at the lengthen/shorten line.

Ladies' Pattern Sizing Chart

Size	Bust Measurement	Hip Measurement	Yardage Needed for Single-Layer Vest (add yardage for more length or fat piping)	Finished Size at Bust and Hips
Small	30" to 32"	32" to 34"	1 yard	37½"
Medium	34" to 36"	36" to 38"	1 yard	41½"
Large	38" to 40"	40" to 42"	1 yard	45½"
Extra-Large	42" to 44"	44" to 46"	1 yard	49½"

Children's Pattern Sizing Chart

Size	Chest Measurement	Yardage Needed for Single-Layer Vest (add yardage for more length or fat piping)	Finished Size at Chest/Waist
Small	23"	⅔ yard	30"
Medium	25"	⅔ yard	33"
Large	27"	≤ 1 yard ¾ of a yard	35½"
Extra-Large	29"	≤ 1 yard ¾ of a yard	37½"

Neckline Design Options

Stand-up collar: Trace the neck edge as is; construct with square or rounded collar.

Jewel neck: Trace the neck edge as is.

V-Neck: Mark a dot on center front 8½" below the center front neck edge on adult sizes or 5½" below center front on children's sizes. Draw a line from dot to the neck shoulder point for V-neck edge

General Cutting Directions

1. Cut out pattern pieces "with nap."

2. Cut out two front pieces and one back (on the fold). Cut the lower edge of the vest on the straight or shirttail cutting line.

3. Cut out the square collar (on the fold) and then trim for a rounded collar, if desired.

And don't forget the Golden Rule for cutting: When cutting a single layer of fabric, always have the fabric right side facing up and the pattern piece right side facing up.

General Sewing Directions

Unless directed otherwise in the project directions, use a ¼" seam allowance.

1. Sew the front pieces to the back, with right sides together, at the shoulder seams.

2. Sew the collar to the neck edge, with right sides together, matching center fronts and center back.

3. Sew the front pieces, with right sides together, to the back at the side seams.

4. Finish the vest with one of the Finishing Options that follow.

Appliqué Embellishment

There is no rule as to whether an appliqué should be on the right or left upper chest/shoulder area. Many times, the appliqué itself is angled in such a manner to make the choice obvious. However, when stitching reverse appliqué, you must plan your appliqué placement before cutting out your garment. (Refer to the Dog Lover's Vest on page 81 for important planning information.)

Finishing Options

Easy Reversible Vest (with exposed seam allowances)

1. Place the main vest against the contrast vest with wrong sides together (finished position).

2. Sew the entire vest outer perimeter and armhole edges using a ½" seam allowance.

3. Trim exposed seam allowance ¼" using a straight or decorative blade.

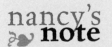

nancy's note

Sewing the seam allowances with a ½" allowance and then trimming to ¼" nets out the same general fit as though the seam allowances had been sewn traditionally (right sides together) using a ¼" seam.

Finishing

Cheater's Wrapped Edge

1. Allow for three 3" x 60" trim strips.

    a. One trim strip will finish both armhole edges.

    b. Two strips, spliced together, will finish the vest outer edges. (Refer to Splicing Trim directions on page 31.)

2. Follow Cheater's Wrapped Edge directions on page 30.

    a. Stitch the trim to the vest using a ⅜" seam allowance (resulting in a ½" finished wrap) for children's garments and ladies' garments that call for a "lighter" touch. Sew with a ⅝" seam allowance (resulting in a ¾" finished wrap) for a sportier edge finish.

    b. Use one-half trim strip per armhole. Begin and end in the underarm area. Splice the trim ends to finish.

    c. Begin and end stitching the trim at vest center back. Splice the trim ends to finish. Before you begin stitching, do a rough measurement around the vest outer edges to plan for the trim splice to be placed between the shoulder seams at the center back neck (or collar) edge.

'Reversible Snaps'

I always smile when someone asks where I found my "reversible snaps," like those featured in the Kid's Reversible Vests on pages 72 through 74.

You don't buy reversible snaps … You make them!

I choose size 20 long-pronged, capped sport snaps from The Snap Source®. (These are available at your favorite local shop or online at www.snapsource.com) The long prongs have terrific holding power, are available in a wide range of colors and have an easy-to-use SnapSetter® attachment.

Now for the "reverse" part: Typically, when you attach sport snaps, you have the pronged decorative cap on the garment right side attached to the socket underneath. Then for the other half of the snap, you have the stud that attaches to the open-prong ring that is on the inside of the garment.

To make the snaps "reversible" (so it doesn't matter what side of the garment is facing out), you simply use another pronged decorative cap instead of the open-prong ring on the underside!

That means you buy twice as many snap sets as you actually use, so you can have that extra decorative cap for the "reverse" side. (But you'll find a lot of practical uses for the remaining "nondecorative" snap sets.) Allow 10 sets (five reversible snaps) for children's sizes and 12 sets (six reversible snaps) for adults' sizes. Snap Placement:

- ½" to ⅝" away from center front edge
- One snap in the center of the stand-up collar, if applicable
- One snap ½" below neck seamline (for smaller children) or ¾" below neck seamline (for larger children and adults)
- One snap 3" above the bottom hemline (for smaller children) or 4" above the bottom hemline (for larger adults)

Evenly space the remaining snaps between the neck and hem snaps.

nancy's note

Whenever I am applying the cheater's wrapped edge finish to a double-layered item that is a print and a solid, I always stitch the trim to the solid side and wrap to the print side. That way, I am trimming the excess on the print side. The print makes the cut edge virtually unnoticeable.

Interfacing or no interfacing?

The "rule" says to insert a piece of interfacing between the fabric layers before attaching snaps on stretch fabric.

To be honest … if I am making the vest for an adult who will either leave it unsnapped or who will snap and unsnap with "reasonable finesse," I don't bother to interface.

However, if the vest is for a kid who snaps and unsnaps with unbridled enthusiasm, I insert a 1½" strip of interfacing between the fleece layers for "security purposes." (Make sure no interfacing peeks out if you are using exposed seam allowances.)

fleece projects

The following pages offer a wide variety of easy-to-sew projects. Look at them as "beginnings". A simple color change can transform a "baby blanket" into a sport throw for the den.

Bunny Ears Blanket

Finished size: as desired

The bunny ears edge finish is a charming variation of the fringed-edge finish. The key to successful bunny ears is a tiny slit. Read on and you'll see what I mean.

The "ear" dimensions can vary, as the fringe can be cut longer and wider for slightly different effects. (Cut fringe longer for flop-eared bunny ears!) Experiment on a scrap of fleece to see what width and length looks best on your fleece weight.

Materials

Fleece yardage sufficient to make blanket size desired.* For the following sizes:

- 36" square or 36" x 45": 1 yard
- 45" square or 45" x 60": 1¼ yards

18mm rotary cutter
Serger tweezers (optional)
*Note: When deciding blanket size, take into account that 4" will be used to make the bunny ears.

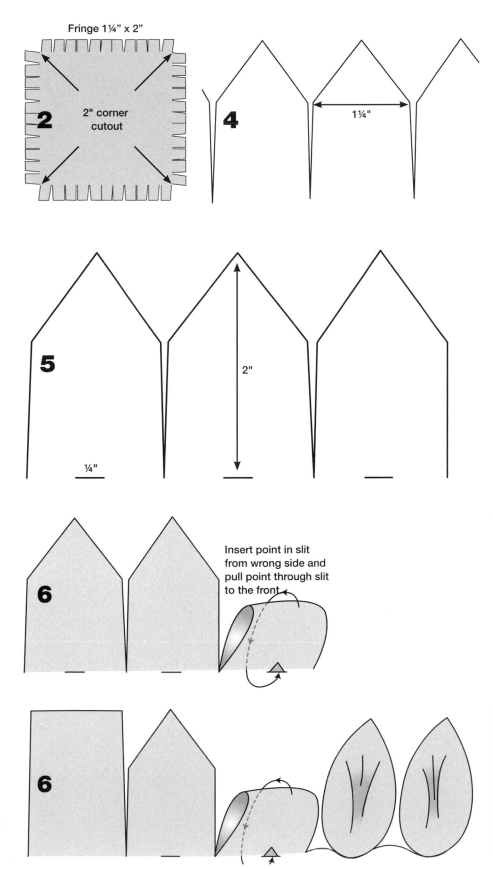

Fringe 1¼" x 2"

2 2" corner cutout

4 1¼"

5 ¼"

2"

6 Insert point in slit from wrong side and pull point through slit to the front

6

Directions

1. Cut the fleece to the desired blanket size (36" square, 36" x 45", 45" square or 45" x 60").

2. Cut out 2" squares from all four of the blanket corners.

3. Quick fringe the blanket edges, cutting the fringe 1¼" wide x 2" long. (Refer to Quick Fringe directions on page 14.)

4. Cut the ends of each fringe-cut into a point. (I call this "picket fencing.") Don't bother to measure; just cut the fringe ends into points. If one point looks a little lopsided, simply recut it.

5. Make a tiny slit at the bottom center of each fringe-cut using an 18mm rotary cutter. (The slit must be tiny, just a nick, maybe ¼". The slit is very narrow, so when the fringe is fed through it, the slit pinches the fleece, puckering it to form a bunny ear.)

6. Insert each fringe point into each slit, feeding from the wrong side and pulling the fringe through the slit to the right side. Pull snugly for a taut finish.

nancy's note

An easy way to pull the picket-fenced fringe through the tiny slit is to insert serger tweezers through the slit, pinch the fringe tip and pull it through.

Ruffle Quilt

Finished size: 45" square

This is a tidy version of the popular rag quilt. It is similar to the rag quilt in that the seam allowances are exposed. However, instead of the exposed seam allowances being cut into fringe, they are precut using the decorative wave blade, which results in a "skinny ruffle" separating each quilt block.

Dimensions and yardage requirements given here are for a simple quilt, with all the rectangles cut the same size. The "quilt blocks" could easily be cut with different dimensions.

Materials Needed

60" fleece solids as follows:
- Color 1 (mint): ⅝ yard
- Color 2 (pink): ⅝ yard
- Color 3 (lilac): ⅓ yard
- Color 4 (yellow): ⅓ yard

Wave decorative rotary blade

Note: Choose one thread that will blend with all or most of the fleece colors. Since the stitches sink into the loft of the fleece, the color does not need to match exactly. I used white thread on this quilt.

Determine Color Scheme

If you are using a color scheme similar to mine, it will be very easy to follow along with my directions and photos. However, if you are choosing a very different color or print scheme, it may get confusing relating your Color 1, 2, 3 and 4 to those pictured here.

Put a sticky note designating your four colors on each one of your colors or prints. Set this labeled set above your work area and constantly refer to it as you follow the directions.

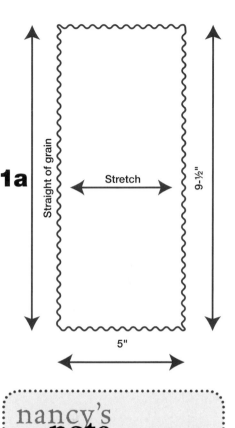

1a

Straight of grain

Stretch

9-½"

5"

Directions

All seam allowances are exposed, sewn with a ¼" seam allowance using a 3.5mm straight stitch length.

1. Use the decorative wave blade to rotary cut the fleece rectangles, as follows:

    a. Cut all rectangles 9½" high x 5" wide. Cut with the longer side (9½") in the direction of least stretch (on the straight of grain).

    b. Cut 13 Color 1 (mint) rectangles.

    c. Cut 13 Color 2 (pink) rectangles.

    d. Cut 12 Color 3 (lilac) rectangles.

    e. Cut 12 Color 4 (yellow) rectangles.

2. Sew a Color 1 (mint) rectangle to a Color 2 (pink), *wrong* sides together, using a ¼" seam allowance and stitching along the long sides.

nancy's note

Cutting the longest side of each block in the direction of least stretch makes it easier to sew the blocks together without distortion.

2

nancy's note

Unlike sewing quilt blocks from a woven fabric, fleece has stretch, so sometimes your blocks and/or rows may be a little uneven at the edges. If that happens, simply use your wave blade and trim to retrue the edges! ("Real" quilters may have a problem with this, but fleece is so easy to work with, why not take advantage of it?)

3. Repeat Step 2 to make 13 Color 1-2 pairs, using the "kite tail" method. When you finish the first pair, position the next pair in place and continue stitching. You will end up with a "kite tail" of 13 pairs. Cut the threads joining the pairs and you are finished in no time!

4. Repeat Steps 2 and 3 for the Color 3 (lilac) to Color 4 (yellow) rectangles to make 12 Color 2-3 pairs.

5. Turn a Color 1-2 square so the rectangles are horizontal, with Color 1 (mint) on top and Color 2 (pink) on the bottom, and pin the edge to the vertical Color 3 (lilac) long side of a Color 3-4 square.

> **a.** Place *wrong* sides together (for exposed seam allowances).
>
> **b.** Finger-press the Color 1-2 block seam allowances open.
>
> **c.** *Always* sew with the horizontal rectangles side facing up. (This makes it easier to keep the finger-pressed exposed seam allowances open.)

6. Refer to the Quilt Layout diagram and continue sewing the quilt blocks together in the same manner as in Step 5 to complete the top row. Finger-press seam allowances open as you go.

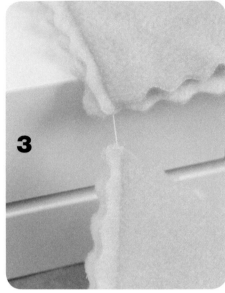

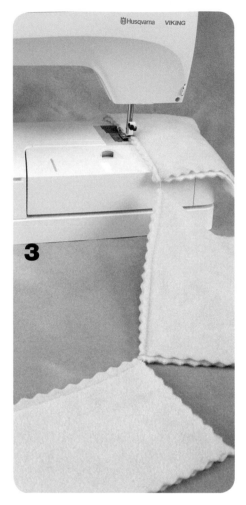

nancy's note

This sounds more complicated than it is! A picture is worth a thousand words. Simply look at the reference photos and do the same thing.

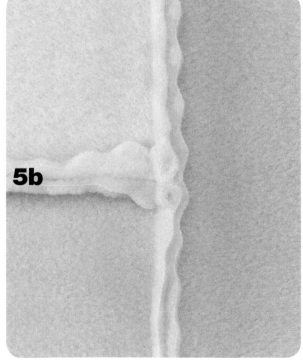

7. Refer to the Quilt Layout to sew Rows 2 through 5.

8. Refer to the Quilt Layout to sew Rows 1 and 2 together.

    a. Place the rows *wrong* sides together.

    b. Finger-press seam allowances open as you go.

    c. Pin the intersections together to make sure they match.

9. Refer to the Quilt Layout to add Rows 3 through 5 to complete the quilt.

10. Retrue the edges by trimming uneven rows with the wave blade, if necessary.

Layout Diagram Key

1 = Color 1	3 = Color 3
2 = Color 2	4 = Color 4

Quilt Layout

Row 1

Row 2

Row 3

Row 4

Row 5

Variation Options

You can easily change the look by changing the colors, including some prints and/or changing the block sizes.

- If using a directional print, make sure all print blocks are laid out in the same direction so all are going in the same direction in the finished blanket.
- Always cut the quilt blocks with the longest edge on the straight of grain, unless, for some reason, your print does not allow this.

Wave Blade vs. Scallop Blade

I used the decorative wave blade, rather than the scallop blade, for very specific reasons:

- The wave blade edge "looks ruffly" and the wavy cut edges do not need to be matched to look good.
- Scallop edges need to be "matched." While the scallops do not look ruffled, they do have a neat look. (Refer to the Striped Scarf project on page 100.) If you want scalloped exposed seam allowances, change the order of cutting and sewing as follows:

a. Cut out the rectangles using the *straight* blade.

b. Sew the rectangles into quilt blocks using a skimpy ⅜" exposed seam allowance.

c. Trim the exposed seam allowance using the scallop blade. Trim the block seam allowances before building the rows.

Lapped-Edge Quilt

Finished size: 50" x 64"

Combine fleece's nonravel characteristic with Wash-Away Wonder Tape and you have a quick-as-a-wink afternoon project!

Materials Needed
Print fleece: ⅝ yard
Color 1 solid fleece (blue): ⅝ yard
Color 2 solid fleece (yellow): ⅝ yard
Color 3 solid fleece (mint): ⅝ yards
Wash-Away Wonder Tape basting tape
Scallop decorative rotary blade
Note: Choose one thread that will blend with all or most of the fleece colors. Since the stitches sink into the loft of the fleece, the color does not need to match exactly. I used white thread on this quilt..

Directions

1. Use the scallop decorative rotary blade to cut rectangles as follows:

a. Cut each fleece piece into two 9½" x 60" pieces.

b. Lay each fleece piece horizontally and cut each into rectangles 9½" high (on the straight of grain, in the direction of least stretch) x 7½" wide. (Read the Caution Before Cutting section before proceeding.)

c. Trim the sides that are "peaked" to make them "scalloped."

2. Lay fleece rectangles in stacks on the cutting table, all with right sides facing up. (You will have a few leftover rectangles.)

a. Print fleece = 14 rectangles

b. Solid 1 fleece (blue) = 14 rectangles

c. Solid 2 fleece (yellow) = 11 rectangles

d. Solid 3 fleece (mint) = 10 rectangles

3. Refer to Determine Color Scheme on page 43 and follow the Quilt Layout diagram here to construct the quilt as follows:

a. Arrange all fleece blocks facing right-side up and start with Row 1. (Refer to page 8 to find the right side of fabric.)

b. Place Wash-Away Wonder Tape along the left edge of the first Color 2 (yellow) block.

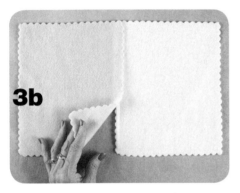

c. Overlap the right edge of the first Color 1 (blue) block ⅜" onto the Color 2 (yellow) block and adhere to the tape.

d. Stitch the blocks together using a serpentine (wavy) stitch. Lengthen and widen the wave stitch to complement the scalloped edge. (Do not be tempted to choose a scallop stitch. The stitched scallop will never match the scallop. The serpentine stitch is much more forgiving.)

e. Refer to the Quilt Layout and continue constructing the top row, always overlapping the leftmost block onto the right block.

f. Repeat Steps 3b through 3e to construct Rows 2 through 7.

g. Place Wash-Away Wonder Tape along the top edge of Row 2.

h. Overlap the Row 1 bottom edge ⅜" onto Row 2 top edge and adhere to tape.

i. Stitch the rows together using a serpentine stitch.

j. Repeat Steps 3g through 3i, overlapping the upper row on the row beneath it, to complete the quilt.

Quilt Layout

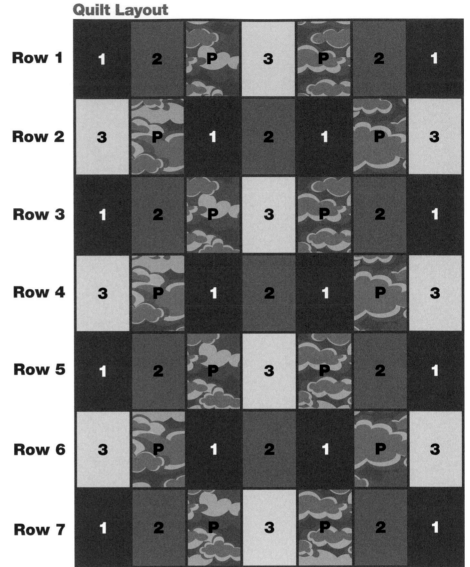

Row 1: 1	2	P	3	P	2	1
Row 2: 3	P	1	2	1	P	3
Row 3: 1	2	P	3	P	2	1
Row 4: 3	P	1	2	1	P	3
Row 5: 1	2	P	3	P	2	1
Row 6: 3	P	1	2	1	P	3
Row 7: 1	2	P	3	P	2	1

Layout Diagram Key
P = Print
1 = Color 1
2 = Color 2
3 = Color 3

nancy's note

Unlike sewing quilt blocks from a woven fabric, fleece has stretch, so sometimes your blocks and/or rows may be a little uneven at the edges. If that happens, simply use your wave blade and trim to retrue the edges!

Framed Baby Blanket

Finished size: 45" x 45"

The "frame" that finished the blanket is a blend of the Reverse Hem and Cheater's Wrapped Edge techniques. A separate fleece strip "frames" the blanket. The blanket itself can be a single or double layer. Since the frame encases the blanket raw edge, a nonfleece fabric could be used for the blanket. The frame *must* be fleece, but the blanket doesn't need to be. If choosing a flannel for the blanket portion, make sure to pre-launder the flannel.

Materials Needed

Main fleece (blanket face): 1¼ yards
Contrast fleece (blanket back): 1¼ yards
Accent fleece (frame strips): ⅞ yard (must be fleece)
Wash-Away Wonder Tape basting tape
Decorative rotary blade
Appliqué scissors (pointed or round-tipped)

Directions

1. Cut the blanket face from the main fleece and the back from the contrast fleece, each 45" square.

2. Cut four 7" x 60" frame strips from the accent fleece. Trim one long edge of each strip using a decorative rotary blade.

3. Place blanket face on top of blanket back, wrong sides together (finished position), and baste layers together at 2½" from the raw edges using a large, long zigzag stitch.

4. Place a strip of Wash-Away Wonder Tape along one side of blanket face, 2¾" from the blanket edge, using the basting stitches as a placement guide. The extra ¼" depth assures that the basting stitches will be covered.

5. Adhere the decorative cut edge of the frame strip to the basting tape, with right sides facing up, allowing the excess strip ends to extend beyond each blanket edge. (Do not trim excess length at this time.)

6. Wrap fleece frame to the blanket back side. Wrap up, over and around blanket raw edges. Adjust wrap for a 3" frame on the blanket face. Pin. (At this point, the frame on the backside will be 4" deep and have a straight cut edge that overlaps the basting stitching approximately 1".)

7. Straight stitch topstitch the frame strip along the decorative edge *beginning and ending* 3" from the ends of the *blanket*. (You are stitching through four layers: Frame strip with decorative edge on top, two blanket layers and the wrapped frame strip on the back.)

nancy's note

For an easy way to baste, use the quilt guide (the slide bar that attaches to the presser foot shank) that came with your machine. Set the guide 2½" away from the needle. If you don't have that accessory, place masking or blue painter's tape on your machine bed 2½" away from the needle.

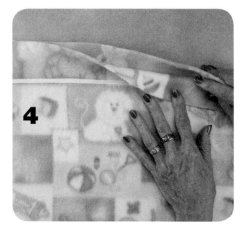

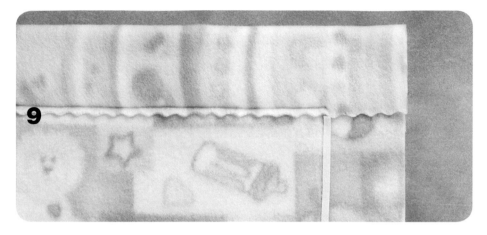

8. Trim excess frame length exactly even with the blanket edges.

9. Place a strip of wash-away basting tape on the next blanket side, 2¾" from the blanket edge, beginning and ending 3" from blanket ends.

10. Repeat Steps 5 and 6 for next blanket edge.

11. Sew the first mitered corner, as follows:

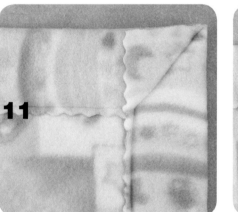

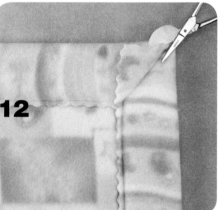

    a. Trim the frame strip extension exactly even with blanket edge.

    b. Make sure the two wrapped frame strips meet snugly at the outside corner.

    c. Sew the miter from the outside corner towards the inner corner of the overlapped frame strips.

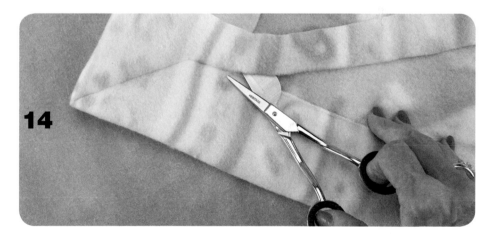

    d. When you get to the inner corner, sink needle, pivot and continue topstitching the next frame strip in place. Stop 3" from the blanket edge.

12. Trim and remove miter wedges on the front and back, leaving a blunt raw-edge mitered seam.

13. Repeat Steps 9, 5 and 6, 11 and 12 for the remaining two edges of the blanket and mitered corners.

14. Trim the excess frame on the blanket back. Trim close to stitching.

nancy's ✿ note

The frame widths can be any depth. Choose a width that complements your blanket size and print scale. Cut the beginning border strips two times the desired visible frame width plus 1". Thus, if you wanted a 2" finished frame, your beginning strip width would be 5", which is a 2" frame width multiplied by 2 (for the wrap) + 1" (for the excess overlap).

Chenille 'BABY' Blanket

Finished size: 45" square

This soft, cuddly baby blanket is embellished with chenille appliquéd letters and finished with the Cheater's Wrapped Edge.

Materials Needed
60" white fleece: 1¼ yards
Pastel fleece in assorted colors:
- two 6" squares (for each letter appliqué)
- ¼ yard (for wrapped edge trim)

Letter Templates on pattern sheet

Directions

1. Cut the white fleece into a 45" square.

2. Trim corners into gently rounded the corners.

3. Make chenille letter appliqués and apply to the blanket. (Refer to Chenille Appliqué directions on page 25.)

> **a.** A, B, C and Y Letter Templates are provided on the pattern sheet for "BABY" or "ABC."

> **b.** The Letter Templates have angled lines to show a suggested placement of the chenille stitching lines for effective slashing. If your stitching lines are at the opposite angle, use these lines as a guide.

> **c.** Refer to main project photo for suggested letter placement.

> **d.** See the Optional Appliqué Ideas for other options.

4. Cut three 3" x 60" pastel fleece trim strips.

5. Splice trim strips together to make one long trim strip. (Refer to Splicing Trim directions on page 31.)

6. Sew trim strip with a ½" seam allowance to the outer edge of the blanket to create the Cheater's Wrapped Edge finish. (Refer to Cheater's Wrapped Edge directions on page 30.)

Optional Appliqué Ideas

- Spell out the baby's name (if it is five letters or less).

- For other letters, choose a collegiate or yearbook font on your computer, block outline. Enlarge the letters to approximately 4" square, or as desired. Print out the letters. Gently round the corners and proceed following the above directions.

- Substitute with the Heart or Star Templates on pattern sheet, and randomly sprinkle them on the blanket.

- Substitute with any simple appliqué motif.

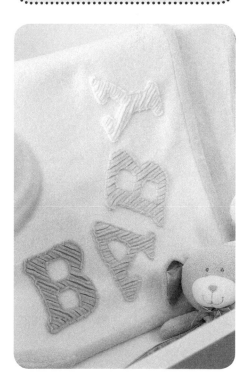

Good Sport T-Shirt Pillow

Looking for something a little different for your favorite athletes?
Surprise them with novelty T-shirt pillows that reflect their favorite sports.

Materials Needed

Commercial T-shirt pattern*
Sport-themed fleece: Per T-shirt pattern fabric requirements
Ribbing: 2½" (for crew neck finish)
Polyester stuffing: 1 pound bag
Hand-sewing needle

*Note: A child's size 4 through 6 makes a middle-size pillow. You could make it an adult size and use as a floor pillow, but you'll need a second bag of stuffing. Choose the size according to the size of pillow you want.

Directions

1. Cut the fleece into the T-shirt front, back and short sleeve pieces per the pattern directions.

2. Trim the back neck edge to be ¾" higher than the pattern front. (Lay the shirt front on top of the shirt back and alter the back neck accordingly.)

3. Sew shoulder seams per the pattern directions.

4. Cut and apply rib trim to neck edge per the pattern directions.

5. Lay T-shirt flat on the table, shoulder seams at the top, with top edge of front ribbing approximately ¼" below the top edge of back ribbing. Pin.

6. Topstitch on the T-shirt front ¼" away from ribbing neck seamline, stitching through both the front and back T-shirt layers. (This closes the neckline, but leaves the ribbing free.)

7. Hand-stitch the top edge of front neck ribbing to the back neck ribbing.

8. Sew the sleeves to the front and back per the pattern directions.

9. Sew the side seams per the pattern directions.

10. Turn under 1" hem on sleeves and pin sleeve hems together, sleeve front to sleeve back. The shoulder seam is at the top and the underarm seam is at the bottom.

11. Topstitch the sleeve hems at ¾", stitching the hem and closing the sleeve lower edge in one step. (You will be sewing through four layers.)

12. Turn under 1" hem on lower edge of T-shirt and pin lower-edge hems together, shirt front to shirt back.

13. Topstitch the lower-edge hem at ¾", stitching the hem and closing the bottom of the shirt in one step. (You will be sewing through four layers.) Leave a 5" opening to insert stuffing.

14. Insert stuffing to desired plumpness.

15. Stitch the lower hem opening closed.

T-shirt patterns vary. Some pattern pieces have the neck edge ready to apply ribbing finish, while other patterns have you trim out the neck edge before applying rib trim. Whichever way your pattern is, trim the back neck edge to be ¾" higher than the front edge. It would fit funny, but this is going to be a pillow, so fit is not an issue!

Shorts Pillow

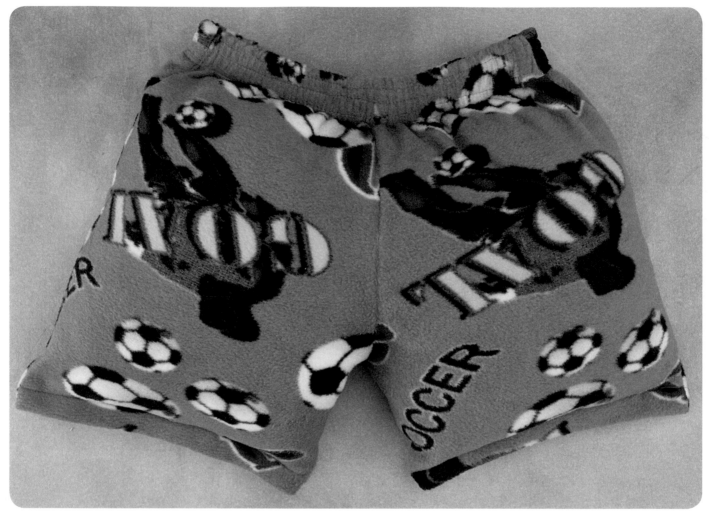

Like the Good Sport T-Shirt Pillow, this project offers another fun way to support your sport.

Materials Needed

Commercial child's sports shorts pattern*
Sport-themed fleece: Per shorts pattern fabric requirements
Sport elastic: Per pattern
Polyester stuffing: 1 pound bag
Hand-sewing needle
Zipper foot

Note: Choose a loose-fitting, fuller-leg sports short pattern with an elastic waist, simple style, and construction. The pillow shown here is a child's size 6.

Directions

1. Cut the fleece into the shorts front and back pieces per the pattern directions.

2. Sew fronts to backs per the pattern directions.

3. Apply waist sport elastic per pattern directions.

4. Pin shorts front to back, matching upper edges of finished elastic waist.

5. Stitch the front to the back using a zipper foot and stitching closely to the lower edge of the encased elastic. (You are stitching through two layers—the front and the back—to close the upper edge of the shorts for stuffing.)

6. Hand-stitch the upper edges of the elastic waist together.

7. Turn under 1" hem at the bottom of each leg and pin the leg hems together, leg front to leg back. The side seam will be at the side edge; inseam may be at the inside edge or offset slightly towards the front, depending upon pattern design.

8. Topstitch the leg hem at ¾", stitching the hem and closing the bottom of the leg in one step. (You will be sewing through four layers.) Repeat on second leg, but leave a 5" opening in the middle of the hem to insert stuffing.

9. Insert stuffing to desired plumpness.

10. Stitch the leg hem opening closed.

nancy's ⁊ note

Stitching the front and back together under the waist elastic and then hand-stitching the upper edges together gives the pillow a defined waist shape.

Sports Blanket and Pillow

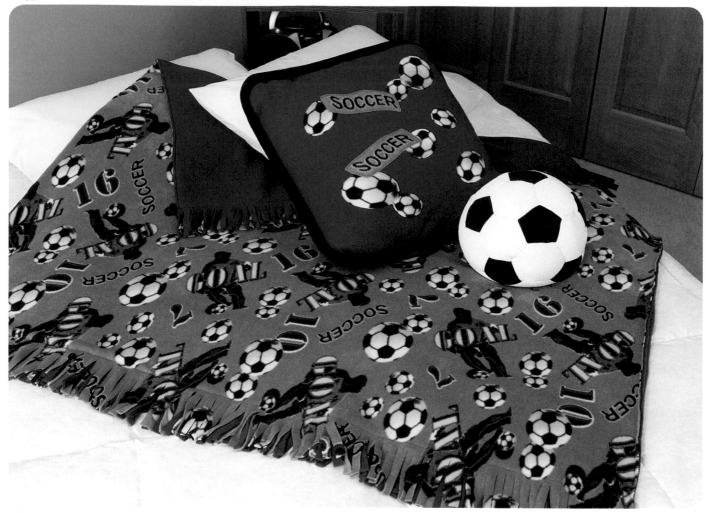

Finished sizes: 60" x 72" blanket; 20" pillow

The blanket and coordinating pillow can be made from all types of prints: sports themes, bright kid prints, soft florals, southwest, nature, etc. Choose a print with a motifs suitable for embellishing a pillow. The larger size blanket with double layer warmth makes the blanket perfect for chasing the chill while sitting in the bleachers cheering for your favorite team. The larger pillow size makes a perfect "TV pillow" for the sport spectator.

Materials Needed*
(add blanket and pillow needs together)
Blanket
Sport-themed print fleece (blanket face): 2 yards
Coordinating solid (blanket back): 2 yards
Note: For a 54" x 60" throw, get 1½ yards each layer.
Pillow
Sport-themed print fleece: enough for appliqués
Coordinating solid (pillow front and back): ⅔ yard
Contrast fleece (fat piping): ¼ yard
20" pillow form
Note: For different pillow sizes and requirements, refer to pages 33 and 35.

Blanket Directions

1. Cut both the print fleece and the coordinating solid fleece into 72" x 60" pieces.

2. Place print and solid fleece layers wrong sides together and pin.

3. Stitch layers together using a ½" seam allowance on the long sides and a 4" seam allowance across the short sides.

4. Use a rotary cutter to trim the blanket close to the stitching on the long sides only.

5. Quick fringe the short sides, cutting the fringe ½" x 4". (Refer to Quick Fringe directions on page 14.)

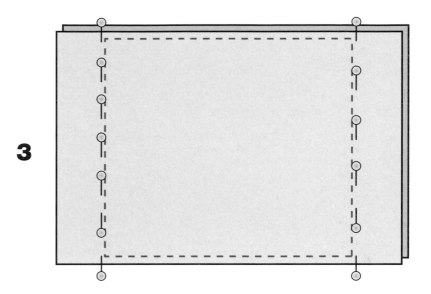

Pillow Directions

Many times you want to make a pillow that coordinates with a blanket, but the print does not offer an "obvious" motif to use. That was the case with this allover print. Each motif, on its own, was too small. Yet, the motifs cut out individually and combined resulted in a great coordinating appliquéd pillow.

1. Refer to Pillow Construction and Cheater's Wrapped Edge/Fat Piping Finish directions on pages 33 and 30 for cutting and sewing directions.

2. Refer to the Blunt-Edge Appliqué Cut-and-Stitch Method on page 16 for appliqué directions.

Double Bunny Ears Round Blanket

Finished sizes (including "ears"): 60" circular (kid) or 54" (baby)

Changing the blanket shape from the traditional square combined with explosive colors took the double bunny ear edge finish from a charming baby blanket to a fun kid blanket. It still is a precious choice for a baby, too, so I included information for a downsized version.

Materials Needed
Baby blanket: 1½ yards for each layer*
Kid blanket: 1¾ yards for each layer*
18mm rotary cutter or blunt-edged buttonhole cutter
Water-soluble pencil
Painter's tape or masking tape (optional)
*Note: Choose two coordinating fleece prints, one print and one solid or two coordinating solids for the two blanket layers.

Stitch Wisdom

This blanket could have been a no-sew project, but a little stitching makes it much easier to cut the fringe.

Quick-fringing on straight edges is a snap. However, when I went to cut 5" fringe-cuts on the circular edge, I found it awkward to determine exactly where the 5" fringe-cuts should begin. The ruler always seemed to be at odd angles. By simply first stitching the layers together with a 5" seam allowance, the stitching line gave me a very defined place to begin each fringe-cut.

Directions

1. Cut each fleece layer into a 54" circle (for baby) or 60" circle (for a child). For an easy way to cut the circles:

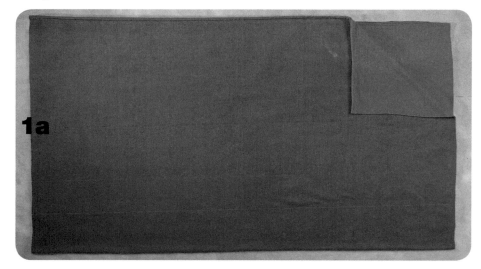

a. Fold full fleece yardage in half. (Baby size will be 27" x 60"; kid size will be 31½" x 60".)

b. Fold the fleece in half again to quarter it. (Baby size will be 27" x 30"; kid size will be 31½" x 30".)

c. In your left hand, hold the beginning of the tape measure at the double-folded point of the fleece, and in your right hand, hold a water-soluble pencil at the 27" mark (radius for a baby blanket) or 30" mark (radius for a kid blanket). Swing in an arc drawing dashed cutting lines for the circle perimeter.

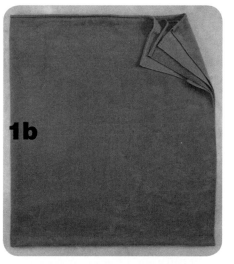

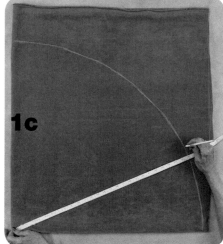

d. Using a 60mm rotary blade (you need the larger blade to cut through the four layers of fleece), cut the drawn arc, but don't unfold it yet.

e. Fold the second fleece layer into quarters, as in Steps 1a and 1b.

f. Lay the still-folded cut first layer on top of the second uncut layer.

g. Using the first layer as a pattern piece, cut the second circle.

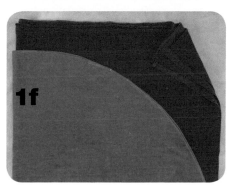

Remember the "old days" when we used to make circle skirts, or round tablecloths using string and a pencil instead of a protractor? This is the same thing.

2. Place the fleece circles *wrong sides together* (finished position) with the *stretches offset.* (It is important to place the greater degrees of stretch in each layer opposite one another. When pulling the bunny ears through the slits, this will prevent the fringe-cuts from stretching out of shape.) Pin. Trim to retrue the edges, as necessary. (Since we will be fringing the outer edges, you don't need to be super-fussy on making sure the circle is perfect.)

3. Sew the blanket layers together using a 5" seam allowance and 3.5mm stitch length.

4. Cut the 5" seam allowance into 2½"-wide (at the seamline) x 5"-long fringe-cuts, cutting through both layers at once.

   a. Because we are working in a circle, the fringe-cuts will be 2½" wide at the base (seamline), but not 2½" wide at the outer edge of the arc. You will need to "fan" each fringe slightly as you cut it. There is not a precise measurement; simply "eyeball" it. If you get off a little here and there, simply realign the ruler and adjust the next fringe angle accordingly. When picket-fenced and pulled through, minor differences will not be visible.

   b. When you are cutting the fringe, stop about 10" before arriving back at the beginning point and measure the remaining distance on the seamline. Adjust remaining fringe-cuts, as necessary, to end up with a full fringe cut.

2

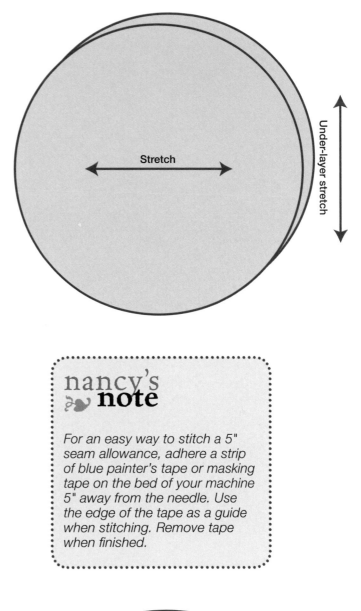

Stretch

Under-layer stretch

nancy's 🦢 note

For an easy way to stitch a 5" seam allowance, adhere a strip of blue painter's tape or masking tape on the bed of your machine 5" away from the needle. Use the edge of the tape as a guide when stitching. Remove tape when finished.

4

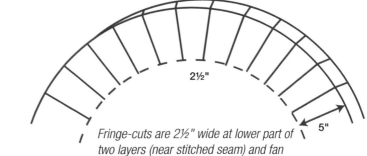

2½"

5"

Fringe-cuts are 2½" wide at lower part of two layers (near stitched seam) and fan out toward the raw edges.

5. Cut the ends of each double-layered fringe cut into a point. I call this "picket fencing." Begin the "picket fence" approximately 2" below the fringed end. Don't measure; just eyeball it. If one point looks a little lopsided, simply recut it. When they are made into the double bunny ears, the slight differences won't be noticeable.

6. Use a small rotary cutter (18mm) or blunt-edged buttonhole cutter to make ½" cuts at the bottom center of each double fringe-cut, cutting on the *fringe side* of the seamline.

7. Pull the double fringe through the slit, from the back to the front, treating the two fringe layers "as one." This is the same process as used in the Bunny Ears Blanket on page 40, except double-layered fringe is pulled through.

6

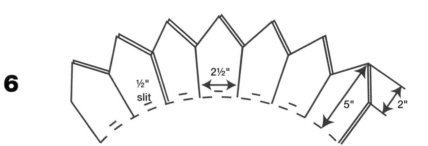

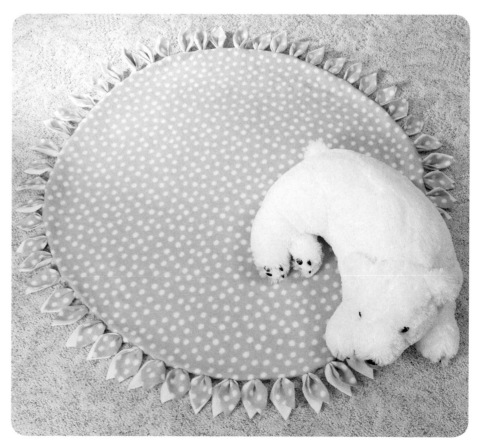

Change the colors to baby pastels, and you have a precious blanket for the littlest member of your family.

Heart Blanket and Coordinating Heart Pillow

Finished sizes: 45" x 56" (blanket); 14" square (pillow)

Reverse Hem, Reverse Appliqué and Fat Piping techniques team up to make this an easy make-in-an-afternoon project. Change the colors to soft pastels and downsize the blanket dimensions, and it is perfect for the littlest family member. Or, choose earth tone colors and a leaf motif, and it is perfect for the family room.

Materials Needed
(add blanket and pillow needs together)
Blanket
Main fleece blanket front (turquoise): 1¼ yards
Contrast fleece blanket back (lime): 1⅜ yards
Clover Mesh Transfer Canvas
Water-soluble pencil
Pillow
Main fleece (turq): ⅜ yard (appliqué and fat piping)
Contrast fleece (lime): ½ yard (pillow front and back)
14" pillow form
Heart Templates on pattern sheet
Note: For different pillow sizes and requirements, refer to pages 33 and 35.

Blanket Directions

1. Cut the main fleece into a 45" x 56" blanket front.

2. Cut the contrast fleece into a 49" x 60" blanket back. (If contrast fleece does not offer a full 60" useable width, reduce blanket front dimensions accordingly, so as to have a blanket front that is 4" smaller than the blanket back.)

3. Arrange the blanket front on top of the blanket back, wrong sides together, with the blanket back 2" larger all around than the blanket front. Trim, if necessary.

4. Finish the outer edges of the blanket with a 2" reverse hem and mitered corners. (Refer to Reverse Hem directions on page 28.)

5. Use the Large Heart and Small Heart Templates (on pattern sheet), Clover Mesh Transfer Canvas and a water-soluble pencil to draw random heart motifs on one side of the blanket (for reverse appliqué). See the picture for suggested arrangement; hearts can be drawn on blanket front or back, whichever color offers best visibility. (Refer to Solid-and-Solid Reverse Appliqué directions on page 21.)

Pillow Directions

1. Cut contrast fleece into pillow front and half-backs for a 14" pillow.

2. Cut main fleece into one 4" x 60" trim strip for fat piping from main fleece

3. Use the Large Heart and Small Heart Templates on pattern sheet, Clover Mesh Transfer Canvas and a water-soluble pencil to draw a small heart within a large heart on contrast fleece. (Refer to page 11.)

4. Cut out the large heart perimeter and edgestitch the appliqué to the center of the pillow front. (Refer to the Cut-and-Stitch Blunt-Edge Appliqué directions on page 16.)

5. Stitch on drawn smaller heart outline.

6. Use appliqué scissors to trim top layer only of inner heart. Discard inner heart. (Refer to Reverse Appliqué on page 21.)

7. Refer to Pillow Construction and Fat Piping Edge Finish directions on page 33 for directions to complete the pillow.

Blooming Blanket

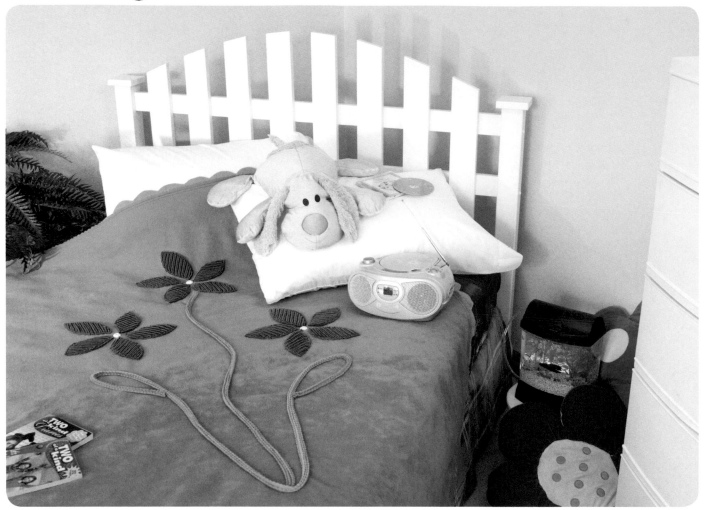

Finished size: 54" x 60"

Embellished with Chenille Appliqué (the flowers) and Chenille Strips (the stems), this blanket takes on the texture of nature.

Materials Needed
Main fleece (blanket): 1½ yards
Contrast 1 fleece (flowers): ⅝ yard
Contrast 2 fleece (stems and scallop border): ⅝ yard
3 buttons, ¾" or ⅞" (flower centers)
Wash-Away Wonder Tape basting tape
Decorative scallop rotary blade
Decorative pinking rotary blade
Appliqué scissors
Fancy Fleece ruler
Flower Petal Template on pattern sheet

Cutting Directions

1. Cut the main fleece in a 54" x 60" blanket piece using the decorative scallop blade. Caution: Do a test cut on a sample fabric to make sure the blade is inserted correctly for a scalloped edge. (Refer to directions on page 12.)

2. Cut Contrast 1 fleece in half, making two 22½" x 30" pieces (for chenille flower appliqués).

3. From Contrast 2 fleece cut four ½" x 60" strips using the decorative pinking blade (for chenille stems).

4. From Contrast 2 fleece cut four 4" x 60" strips. Use the Fancy Fleece ruler to trim one long side of each strip, creating a scalloped edge.

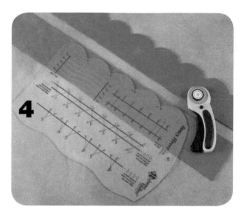

Directions

1. Make Chenille Appliqués from Contrast 1 fleece. (Refer to Chenille Appliqué directions on page 25.)

2. Cut out 15 chenille flower petal appliqués, using the template on pattern sheet. You may keep the chenille lines angled the same direction for all petals, or vary them as desired.

3. Lay the blanket piece on the floor and arrange three five-petal flowers as desired. (Refer to the main project photo for suggested placement.)

4. Stitch appliqués in place and trim edges as needed. (Refer to Chenille Appliqué directions on page 25.)

5. Sew buttons in place to create the flower centers.

6. Make two chenille strips for the stems. (Refer to Chenille Strips directions steps 1 through 5 on page 27.)

7. Lay the blanket on the floor and arrange the chenille strips, as desired, to create winding vines and simplistic leaf outlines. (Refer to the main project photo for suggested placement.)

8. Peel off paper backing from the basting tape and adhere chenille strip stems and leaves. Stitch to secure. (Refer to Chenille Strips directions, Steps 6 through 7 directions on page 27.)

9. Sew scallop border trim to the blanket edge, as follows:

a. With right sides facing up, lay the blanket on one piece of scallop border trim so the blanket edge is ½" above the top slit of the border scallop. Begin at one corner of the blanket, aligning the beginning of one full large scallop to the edge of the blanket. Pin. (At the opposite corner, you should end with one full large scallop. If necessary, trim blanket a little to fit.)

b. Topstitch the blanket to the border trim, stitching ¼" away from blanket edge.

c. Topstitch again, ¼" away from first stitching line.

d. On wrong side of blanket, use appliqué scissors to cut away excess border trim close to the innermost stitching line.

e. Repeat Steps 9a through 9d for the remaining three sides of the blanket.

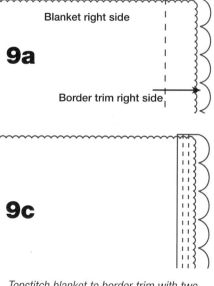

Topstitch blanket to border trim with two lines of stitching spaced ¼" apart.

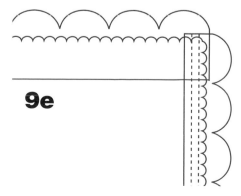

Heart Nine-Patch Quilt

Finished size: 44" square

Large patches and large appliqués in fresh bright colors are sure to be a hit with any young girl. Looking for a mom-and-me project? This one would be fast and easy. (The "and me" part of the duo actually could do most of it herself!)

Materials Needed

Color 1 solid fleece (purple): ⅞ yard
Color 2 solid fleece (turquoise): ½ yard
Color 3 solid fleece (pink): ¼ yard
Wash-Away Wonder Tape basting tape
Temporary adhesive spray
Decorative wave blade
Heart Template on pattern sheet

Directions

1. Use the decorative wave blade to cut pieces, as follows:

- five 15" squares from Color 1 fleece

- four 15" squares from Color 2

- five Heart appliqués from Color 3 (Heart Template found on pattern sheet.)

2. Spray temporary adhesive lightly onto the wrong side of each Heart appliqué and adhere to the centers of all Color 1 squares.

3. Stitch heart appliqué to fleece square topstitching ¼" away from wavy cut edge of appliqué.

Quilt Layout

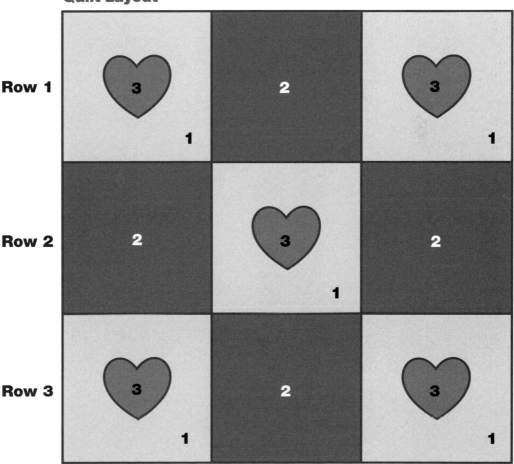

Layout Diagram Key
1 = Color 1
2 = Color 2
3 = Color 3

4. Refer to Determine Color Scheme on page 43 and follow the Quilt Layout diagram here to construct the quilt, as follows:

a. Arrange all fleece blocks facing right-side up and start with Row 1. (Refer to page 8 to find the right side of fabric.)

b. Place Wash-Away Wonder Tape along the left edge of the first Color 2 (turquoise) block.

c. Overlap the right edge of the first Color 1 (purple) block ⅜" onto the Color 2 (turquoise) block and adhere to the tape.

d. Stitch the blocks together using a serpentine (wavy) stitch. Lengthen and widen the wave stitch to complement the wavy fleece edge.

e. Refer to the Quilt Layout and finish the top row as in Steps 4b through 4d, overlapping the leftmost block on the right block.

f. If edges of quilt blocks are uneven, simply trim with the wave blade to retrue.

g. Repeat Steps 4b through 4e to construct Rows 2 and 3.

h. Place Wash-Away Wonder Tape along the top edge of Row 2.

i. Overlap the Row 1 bottom edge ⅜" onto Row 2 and adhere to tape.

j. Stitch the rows together using a serpentine stitch.

k. Repeat Steps 4h through 4j to sew Row 3 to Row 2.

Trucks-and-Planes Reversible Vest

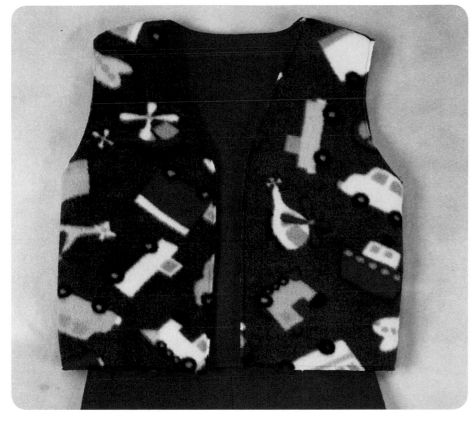

This vest—and those that follow— were made using the multisized vest pattern found at the back of the book. Although they all feature exposed raw-edge seams (because it is the quickest), they could have been finished with the Cheater's Wrapped Edge finish, as shown on the ladies' vest on pages 81 through 84.

This vest uses a straight-edged blade, suitable for the males in the family.

Materials Needed
Vest

Main fleece (print): Per Children's Pattern Sizing Chart on page 36
Contrast fleece (red solid): Per Children's Pattern Sizing Chart on page 36
Straight edge rotary blade

Vest Directions

1. Cut out vest pieces from both the main fleece and contrast fleece per the General Cutting Directions on page 37. (Also note the Neckline Design Options V-Neck directions on page 36.)

2. Sew the vest. (Refer to General Sewing Directions and Easy Reversible Vest directions on page 37.)

3. Choose motifs for Reverse Appliqué on the left front (as when wearing) print side. (Refer to the main project photo for suggested placement.)

4. Create the Reverse Appliqué motifs. (Refer to Print-and-Solid Reverse Appliqué directions on page 20.)

Reversible Floral Vest and Braided Scarf

Here, the exposed seam allowances were trimmed with the decorative scallop blade to make the floral print even more feminine. (Refer to Multisized Vest Pattern and General Sewing Information on pages 36 through 37 for sizing and pattern information.)

Materials Needed

Vest

Main fleece (bright floral print): Per Children's Pattern Sizing Chart on page 36

Contrast fleece (coordinating print or solid): Per Children's Pattern Sizing Chart on page 36

10 to 12 sets* long-pronged, size 20 Sport Snaps

Decorative scallop (or wave) blade

Vest Pattern (enclosed at back of book)

Braided Scarf

Main fleece: ⅛ yard

Contrast fleece: ⅛ yard

Accent fleece: ⅛ yard

Note: 10 to 12 Sport Snaps sets is not a misprint. Smaller children's sizes will need 10 sets; larger children's sizes need 12 sets. You need twice as many snap sets than you can see on the vest since it is reversible. Refer to Reversible Snaps on page 38 for explanation.

Vest Directions

1. Cut out vest pieces from both main fleece and contrast fleece per the General Cutting Directions on page 37.

2. Sew the vest. (Refer to General Sewing Directions and Easy Reversible Vest directions on page 37.)

3. Finish the vest front edges with snaps. (Refer to Reversible Snaps directions on page 38.)

Braided Scarf Directions

Refer to Braided Scarf directions on page 102.

Pants Option

Purchase additional contrast yardage and make coordinating pants using a simple, pull-on, elastic-waist purchased pants pattern.

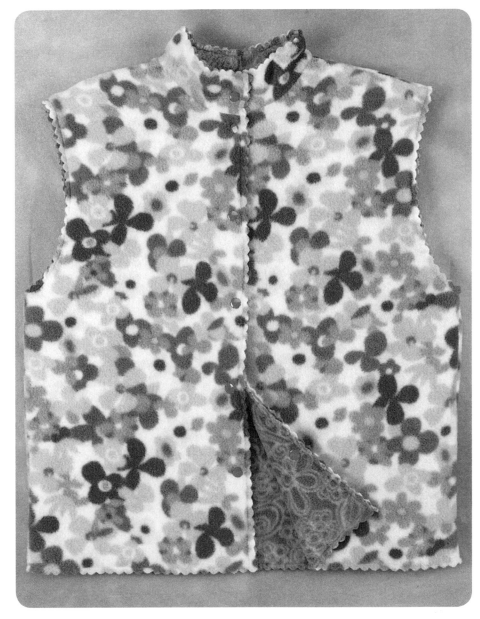

Discover the Possibilities

In addition to the model garments shown here, any of the following options could have been chosen:

- Rounded stand-up collar

- No collar (just a jewel-neck edge)

- V-neck version

- Trimmed with a straight blade or decorative wave blade

Circles-and-Dots Reversible Vest and Scarf

The vest here again is reversible, giving your favorite little lady two ways to wear her outfit! The solid vest is embellished using the Reverse Appliqué technique. The scarf is a trendy addition to the outfit that is both fashionable and warm. And the pants shown in the photo can easily be made by purchasing a commercial pants pattern and following those instructions.

Materials Needed
Vest
Main fleece (bright print): Per Children's Pattern Sizing Chart on page 36
Contrast fleece (purple solid): Per Children's Pattern Sizing Chart on page 36
Decorative wave (or scallop) blade
10 to 12 sets* long-pronged, size 20 Sport Snaps
Vest Pattern (enclosed at back of book)
Scarf
Main fleece: ¼ yard
Contrast fleece: ¼ yard
*Note: 10 to 12 Sport Snaps sets is not a misprint. Smaller children's sizes will need 10 sets; larger children's sizes need 12 sets. You need twice as many snap sets than you can see on the vest since it is reversible. (Refer to Reversible Snaps on page 38 for explanation.)

Vest Directions

1. Cut out vest pieces from both the main fleece and contrast fleece per the General Cutting Directions on page 37.

2. Sew the vest. (Refer to General Sewing Directions and Easy Reversible Vest directions on page 37.)

3. Choose motifs for Reverse Appliqué on the right front (as when wearing) print side. (Refer to main project photo for suggested placement.)

4. Create the Reverse Appliqué motifs. (Refer to Print-and-Solid Reverse Appliqué directions on page 20.)

5. Finish the vest front edges with snaps. (Refer to Reversible Snaps directions on page 38.)

Scarf

1. Cut both the main fleece and contrast fleece into scarf lengths. For a young child, cut each layer 9" x 48". For an older child, each layer begins at 9" x 60".

2. Place main fleece and contrast fleece scarf strips wrong sides together.

3. Cut both scarf ends into squared angles, as shown in the photo.

4. Stitch scarf layers together using a ½" seam allowance.

5. Trim exposed seam allowances using the decorative blade.

6. Create the Reverse Appliqué motifs after scarf is sewn. (Refer to Print-and-Solid Reverse Appliqué directions on page 20.)

Easy Reversible Vest

Materials Needed

Main fleece (print or solid): Per Ladies' Pattern Sizing
Chart on page 36
Contrast fleece (solid): Per Ladies' Pattern Sizing
Chart on page 36
Decorative wave blade
Vest Pattern (enclosed at back of book)

Directions

1. Cut out vest pieces from both the main fleece and contrast fleece per the Cutting Directions on page 37. (Also note the V-Neck Neckline Design Options directions on page 36, if desired.)

2. Sew the vest. (Refer to General Sewing Directions and Easy Reversible Vest directions on page 37.)

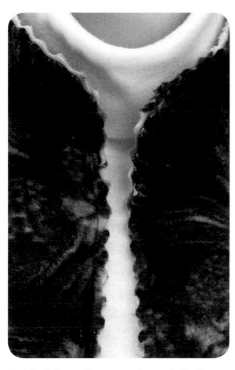

Detail of decorative wave edge on both the vest front and collar.

Chenille-Yoked Vest

Instead of being reversible like the vest before it, this vest uses the under-layer to create a chenille yoke..

Materials Needed

Main fleece (print or solid): Per Ladies' Pattern Sizing Chart on page 36 (plus ¼ yard if used for trim)*
Contrast fleece (solid): Per Ladies' Pattern Sizing Chart on page 36 (plus ¼ yard if used for trim)*
Vest Pattern (enclosed at back of book)

*Note: The fat piping finishing trim can be made from either the main or contrast fleece. Decide which trim fabric you prefer and add ¼ yard to that fabric's requirements.

Directions

Important caution: When cutting the back and collar in Steps 1 and 2, leave larger-than-needed pieces for vest fronts. (To use in Step 3.)

1. Cut out one vest back and one rounded collar each from both the main fleece and contrast fleece. Do *not* cut the vest fronts at this time.

2. Cut three 3" x 60" trim strips on the crossgrain from the desired fleece.

3. On the right side of the *contrast* fleece:

> **a.** Draw a rough outline of the left and right vest fronts. (Draw one vest front. Flip the pattern piece over to draw the opposite front.)

> **b.** Leave as large a space as possible surrounding each vest outline.

> **c.** On both drawn fronts, mark a dot on the center front 13" below the neck edge. Draw a yoke line from the marked dot to the armhole, creating this line at a 45-degree angle to center front. (Use angle marking on your acrylic ruler as a guide.)

> **d.** Draw parallel rows spaced 3" apart above the yoke line.

4. Cut out "matching-sized" *main* fleece pieces for each "drawn" contrast fleece front.

5. Place the drawn solid fleece on top of the print fleece with wrong sides together. (If the print is directional, make sure the print is in the correct position.) Pin.

6. Beginning on the yoke line, stitch chenille rows using the drawn parallel lines as a guide. (Refer to Chenille Yardage directions—Steps 1 and 2 only—on page 23, but do not slash the channels yet.)

The main fleece can be either a print or a solid. The contrast fleece (under-layer) is always a solid fleece.

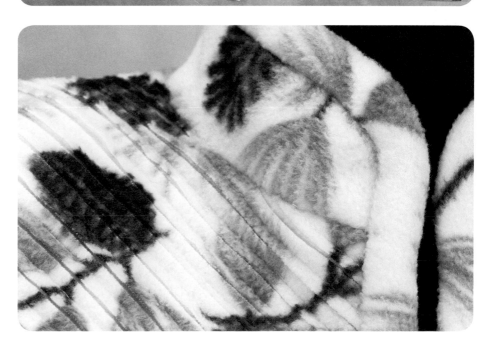

3-6

7. Cut out vest fronts from the chenille-stitched fabric, as follows:

a. Cut out one vest front. Gently round the center front lower edge.

b. Flip over the "just cut out front" and use it as the pattern piece to cut out the opposite front, matching the bottom chenille stitching lines.

8. Slash channels open to create chenille. Slash on the main fleece side. (Refer to Chenille Yardage directions—Step 3—on page 24.)

9. Construct the vest, treating the double-layered fronts, back and collar "as one piece."

a. Baste layers together around outer edges, using a large, long zigzag stitch. Keep the basting stitches within the ¼" seamline area. On the vest fronts, baste the vest outer edges in the area beneath the chenille stitching.

b. Baste collar pieces with wrong sides together (finished position),.

c. Sew the vest fronts to the back at the shoulders, with right sides together, using a ¼" seam allowance. (Shoulder seams have four layers.)

d. Sew the collar to the neck edge, with right sides together, matching the center fronts and center backs. (Neck seam has four layers.)

10. Finish the vest with a Cheater's Wrapped Edge finish. (Refer to Cheater's Wrapped Edge on page 38.)

7b

Dog Lover's Vest and Coordinating Knitted Scarf

This is a reversible vest with two distinctive different looks. The knitted scarf is an "exact match" because the yarn is made from the fleece print! I called it a "Dog Lover's Vest" simply because of the print. It could be a Flower Lover's Vest or a Horse Lover's Vest, depending upon the print. The print will dictate whether the Reverse Appliqué technique (page 20) or the Blunt-Edge Appliqué technique (page 16) would be better. If you can easily lay out your vest front and place the chosen print motif in the proper area (in this instance, upper chest/shoulder area) and the motif outline is simple, then Reverse Appliqué is suitable. If the print motif is difficult to place properly, then use the Blunt-Edge Appliqué (as shown in the Nature Vest on page 84). The motifs on this print were easy to work with, so the Reverse Appliqué technique worked well.

Materials Needed

Vest
Main fleece (print): Per Ladies' Pattern Sizing Chart on page 36
Fleece contrast (solid): Per Ladies' Pattern Sizing Chart on page 36
Fleece accent (for trim): ¼ yard
Vest Pattern (enclosed at back of book)

Scarf
Main fleece (print): 1 yard*
Size 13 (9.0mm) knitting needles
Transparent ruler

*Note: The fleece yardage for the scarf is a tough one to be specific on. How large are the needles? How tight is your gauge? How intricate is your design? 1 yard should yield a medium width, medium length scarf.

Caution Before Cutting

Before cutting out the print vest, choose the motif you want for the reverse appliqué. To get the chosen motif placed correctly in the finished reversible vest (it will show when the solid side is worn facing out), cut out each of the vest print front pieces a single layer at a time, with right side of fleece facing up.

If your motif is on the right shoulder area of the print front (right as when wearing), it will show on the left shoulder when worn solid side-out. There is no hard-and-fast rule as to whether the appliqué should be on the right or the left. If you have a preference, the time to watch carefully is during the cutting stage.

On the pattern included at the back of the book, I find it very helpful to write "left front" on the traced pattern piece, and then flip the pattern piece over and write "right front." At a glance, these words tell me that, when cutting out single-layer fabric with right side facing up, if the words read "right front," I am cutting the vest right front; if the words read "left front," I am cutting the vest left front.

Vest Directions

1. Cut out vest pieces from both the main fleece and contrast fleece per the General Cutting Directions on page 37.

2. Sew the vest. (Refer to General Sewing Directions and Easy Reversible Vest directions on page 37.)

3. Pin around the outline of the chosen appliqué motif with print side facing up. (Refer to main project photo for suggested placement.)

4. Create the Reverse Appliqué motif. (Refer to Print-and-Solid Reverse Appliqué directions on page 20.)

5. Finish the vest with a Cheater's Wrapped Edge finish. Apply trim to the solid side and wrap to the print side. (Refer to Cheater's Wrapped Edge on page 38.)

Scarf Directions

In the Easy Appliquéd Cape project on page 86, you make a piece of fleece yarn that is couched in place as a vine for the appliquéd leaves. Well, fleece yarn for knitting (or crocheting) is the same thing, except we are going to create one long, continuous strand, rather than tie a lot of individual strands together for the necessary length.

Making Fleece Yarn

1. Trim and remove the selvages from both edges of the fleece.

2. Use a transparent ruler and straight edge rotary blade to make ½" cuts on the crossgrain (the 60" width; direction of most stretch), stopping ½" from each end.

3. Beginning at the upper left corner, extend the first cut entirely through the ½" uncut edge. (This gives you a starting point for making one long fleece strip.)

4. Cut through the uncut side edges, alternating sides to make one long, continuous fleece zigzag strip.

5. Grab one end of the continuous zigzag fleece strip between your pinched fingers, stretching the fleece firmly. The fleece will curl and form a yarn. Keep pulling until the entire zigzag strip has been stretched into one long piece of fleece yarn.

6. Knit into desired scarf (or hat).

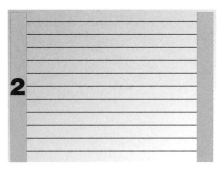

nancy's note

If you happen to goof and cut through the end in Step 2 of the Scarf Directions, don't worry. After you stretch the fleece into the yarn, you can tie the pieces together.

For wonderful knitted scarf patterns, check out Knit Ponchos, Wraps & Scarves *by Jane Davis, and for knitted hat patterns, see* Quick Knits with Today's Yarns *by Jane S. Davis. Both books, published in 2005, are available through Krause Publications either at www.krausebooks.com or by calling the customer service number listed on page 2.*

Nature Vest

As I stated, Blunt-Edge Appliqué allowed me to choose a variety of appliqué motifs and place them exactly where I wanted them. As stated in Dog Lover's Vest on pages 81 and 82, the print dictates whether you should choose the Blunt-Edge Appliqué or Reverse Appliqué technique. The nature print offered a variety of motifs for appliqué, but were not necessarily where I wanted them. I wanted two appliqués on the vest front and one on center back. To attempt arranging placement of all the motifs during the pattern layout and cutting stages would have been impossible. It was much easier to choose the motifs individually and Blunt-Edge Appliqué them in the desired locations.

Materials Needed

Main fleece (print): Per Ladies' Pattern Sizing Chart on page 36 (plus extra yardage for appliqué motifs)
Contrast fleece (solid): Per Ladies' Pattern Sizing Chart on page 36
Accent solid fleece (trim): ¼ yard
Vest Pattern (enclosed at back of book)

Directions

1. Cut out vest pieces from both the main fleece and contrast fleece per the General Cutting Directions on page 37. (Refer to the V-Neck Neckline Design Options directions on page 36.) Gently curve the lower center front corners.

2. Choose the appliqué motifs and determine placement. (Refer to main project photo for placement ideas.)

3. Stitch appliqués to the solid vest. (Refer to either the Cut-and-Stitch or Stitch-and-Cut Blunt-Edge Appliqué methods on pages 16 and 17.)

4. Sew the vest. (Refer to General Sewing Directions and Easy Reversible Vest directions on page 37.)

5. Finish the vest with a Cheater's Wrapped Edge finish. Apply trim to the solid side and wrap to the print side. (Refer to Cheater's Wrapped Edge on page 38.)

The back of the solid side of the vest features an appliqué motif, too.

nancy's note

The nature motifs had "busy" edges, so I used the Stitch-and-Cut Method. I cut out the motifs approximately 1" bigger than the actual motif edges, stitched them in place and then trimmed the excess.

Easy Appliquéd Cape

This simple cape is a fun accessory when the weather requires just a little something to ward off the chill. The vine is fleece yarn accented with Blunt-Edge Appliqué leaves.

Materials Needed

Main fleece: 2-¼ yards
Contrast 1 solid fleece (leaf appliqués): ⅓ yard
Contrast 2 solid fleece (vine)*: 1" x 60"
Clover Mesh Transfer Canvas
Water-soluble pencil
Appliqué scissors (pointed or round-tipped)
Braiding presser foot (optional)
Leaf Template = on pattern sheet
Vest Pattern (enclosed at back of book)

*Note: There is no misprint in that you only need 1" of fleece to make the vine. If you need to purchase fleece, an ⅛ yard cut is generally the smallest amount a store will cut. However, if you have short scraps in your stash, you can make shorter vines, beginning and ending under leaf appliqués.

Cutting Directions

Cape

1. Cut the main fleece into a 58" x 78" rectangle.

2. Fold the rectangle in half lengthwise to create a double-layer 29" x 78" rectangle.

3. Cut out the cape according to the Cape Layout diagram, gently rounding the corners. (Center front opening and rounded outer corners are designated by the broken lines.)

Fleece Vine

1. Cut the Contrast 2 solid fleece into an exact ⅜" wide x 60" long (or shorter pieces, if working from your stash).

2. Trim and remove selvages.

3. Grab one end of the fleece strip and pull the strip between pinched fingers, stretching the fleece tightly. The fleece will curl and form a yarn.

Leaf Appliqués

1. Cut 12 Contrast 1 solid fleece 6" square appliqué pieces.

2. Use Clover Mesh Transfer Canvas and a water-soluble pencil to trace one leaf with stem onto the right side of each appliqué piece, using the Leaf Template = on pattern sheet. Do not cut out the individual leaves. (Refer to Mesh Transfer Canvas directions on page 11.)

Cape Layout

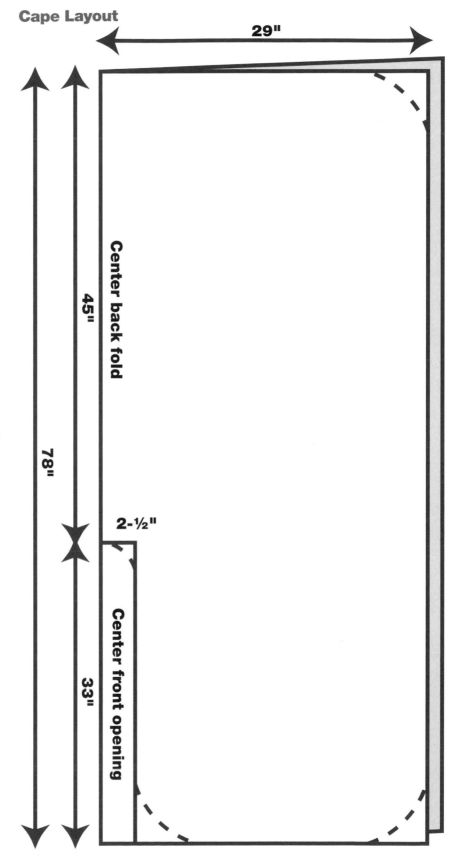

Sewing Directions

1. Fold up a ½" hem allowance on all cut edges of the cape.

2. Topstitch the hem in place, sewing from the wrong side, using a ⅜" seam allowance. (Stitch from the wrong side because it is much easier to see and maintain an even hem allowance.)

3. Lay the fleece yarn along the lower and front edges of the cape, creating a gently wandering vine. The vine goes from one lower front edge, up around the neck, and back to the other front lower edge. Loosely pin in place. (Refer to main project photo for suggested vine placement.)

4. Stitch vine to the cape using a 4mm wide and 4mm long zigzag stitch and thread to match the vine color in the needle. Adjust the stitch width as necessary to clear the yarn on both sides of the zigzag stitch.

5. Place the traced leaf appliqué patches in a random, balanced arrangement and pin in place.

6. Use a 3mm-long straight stitch and matching thread in the needle to stitch around the leaf outline, veins and stem.

7. Use appliqué scissors to trim excess fleece close to the stitching.

nancy's note

If you have a braiding presser foot, insert the fleece yarn through the hole on the top of the foot. The hole efficiently guides the yarn for accurate stitch placement.

Checkerboard Poncho

I cheated a little by including this project in a 90-minute project book. It does take longer than 90 minutes, but not nearly as long as you might think—maybe two-and-a-half or three hours. This easy-to-make poncho features a three-color combination with the "main" color going up the center front, framing the face, and returning down the center back. You could make this a two-color poncho, a three-color poncho using a totally different color arrangement, or a multicolor poncho with random color squares.

Materials Needed

Color 1 main fleece (rust) (center front and back squares, neck opening, squares and fringe): 1⅓ yards
Color 2 contrast fleece (sage) (squares and fringe): 1⅓ yards
Color 3 accent fleece (taupe) (squares): ⅔ yard
Contrast thread for exposed seam blanket stitching*
Pattern tracing paper
Water soluble pencil
Neck Template on pattern sheet
*Note: Black is a great color choice for the contrast thread.

Directions

1. Cut the fleece.

  a. From main fleece Color 1 (rust), cut:
   - 10 12" squares
   - four 6" x 60" fringe-cuts

  b. From contrast fleece Color 2 (sage), cut:
   - 10 12" squares
   - four 6" x 60" fringe-cuts

  c. From accent fleece Color 3 (taupe), cut six 12" squares.

Caution Before Cutting

The directions call for 12" squares. You will get five squares from ⅓ yard (12") of 60" fleece. Most fleeces are 60" or even wider, but sometimes they are narrower.

Before you begin cutting the squares, trim the selvages and measure the fleece width of all three colors. If all are 60" or wider, go ahead and cut your 12" squares. If any piece is less than 60", adjust all your square sizes accordingly to get five squares across the width of the fabric. Cut all squares the narrower width.

Example: Your fleece only measures 58", so divide 58" by 5 for 11.6". That's the size your squares need to be to yield five squares across. (But make it easy on yourself and simply cut 11½" squares.)

This poncho has no critical fit issues. A slightly smaller square is not going to make any difference.

Color 1 Square

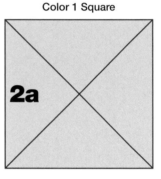

2. Create the neck opening.

  a. Use a water-soluble pencil to draw lines from corner to corner on the wrong side of a Color 1 square, marking the center intersection.

  b. Place a second Color 1 square, right sides together, against the marked square. Arrange the squares so the greatest degree of stretch on each layer is opposite the other. (This offset stabilizes the neck opening.)

  c. Trace the Neck Template on pattern sheet onto a piece of paper to make a pattern piece for cutting the neck opening.

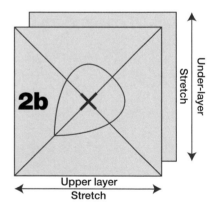

Under-layer Stretch

Upper layer Stretch

  d. Place the Neck Template on marked Color 1 square pair, aligning center marks. Make sure the point of the V-neck is aimed directly at a corner. Pin.

  e. Cut around the template neck edge, cutting through both layers, to create a neck opening.

  f. Sew the neck opening with a ¼" seam allowance. Begin and end the stitching at the center back. Pivot at the point of the V.

  g. For ease in turning, clip to the stitching line at the point of the V. Be careful not to cut through the stitches.

  h. Turn the neck opening center squares right sides out. Pin.

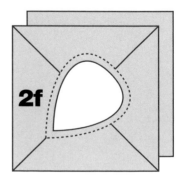

  i. With matching thread in the needle, topstitch the neck opening at ¼", beginning and ending the stitching at the center back and pivoting at the V.

  j. Topstitch a second time, ¼" away from first stitch line.

  k. Pin the outer edge of the neck squares together. Trim edges, as necessary, to neaten and retrue.

3. Set up your machine.

a. Place black or contrast thread in the needle and bobbin.

b. Select a blanket stitch on your machine, setting the stitch length for a *minimum* stitch of 4mm long and 4mm wide.

c. Touch the mirror-image (side-to-side) function on your machine to change the blanket stitch back and forth to accommodate your needs, seaming or appliqué.

4. Construct the poncho, as follows:

a. Construct Row 1 using blanket stitch A (in the Nancy's Note illustration). With *wrong* sides *always* together (all seam allowances will be exposed):

- Stitch Color 2 to Color 1.
- Stitch Color 2-1 pair to C3.
- Follow the Poncho Layout diagram on page 92 to finish Row 1.

b. Row 2: Stitch row same as Row 1 using the Poncho Layout as your color sequence guide.

c. Row 3: (This is the center row which includes the neck opening.) With *wrong* sides *always* together (all seam allowance will be exposed):

- Stitch Color 3 to Color 2.
- Stitch Color 3-2 pair to the Color 1 double-layer neck opening square. Carefully refer to photo and Poncho Layout and make sure the V-point of the neck opening will be pointing towards the Color 1 (main color) squares that run from center front to center back.
- Follow the Poncho Layout to finish Row 3.

d. Row 4: Follow the Poncho Layout to construct row 4.

e. Row 5: Follow the Poncho Layout to construct Row 5.

f. Trim rows, as necessary, to neaten and retrue the edges.

g. Construct poncho by sewing the rows together using blanket stitch A. With *wrong* sides *always* together (all seam allowance will be exposed) and matching seams:

- Sew the bottom of Row 1 to the top of Row 2.
- Sew the bottom of Row 2 to the top of Row 3. (First double-check to make sure the V-point of the neckline is pointing in the correct direction. If not, you still have time to easily tear out stitches and correct.)
- Continue in the same manner for remaining rows.
- Trim outer edges of poncho, as necessary, to neaten and retrue the edges.

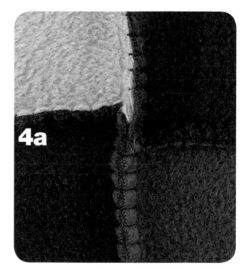

Double-check: The straight stitches are on the left (¼" seam) and the "swing" stitches are to the right, jumping over the aligned raw edges. All seam allowances are exposed and blanket-stitched.

5. Create the fringe trim. You are going to make one long (6" x 240") double-layered fringe trim strip, so determine which color you prefer as the top layer of trim. The model garment (and directions) are given using Color 2 (sage) as the top layer and Color 1 (rust) as the under-layer. Adjust accordingly if you are choosing otherwise.

    a. With right sides facing up, place Color 2 fringe-cut on top of Color 1 fringe-cut.

    b. Slide Color 2 over ½" to make a ½" offset at both ends of the trim strip.

    c. Baste layers together on one long side using a 1" seam allowance. Stop basting stitches 2" from the end.

    d. With right sides facing up, butt the next double-layer set of fringe trim strips to the ends of basted fringe strips. (The offset ends make it easy to connect the fringe-cuts.)

    e. Continue basting with the 1" seam allowance, again stopping 2" before the end.

    f. Repeat steps 5a through 5e to join the third and fourth double-layers of fringe trim strips, finishing with one long (approximately 6" x 240") basted double-layer trim strip.

    g. Trim the ½" offset ends of strips, making the strip ends even.

    h. Use the basted seamline as a stopping point and cut fringe 5" long x ½" wide along the entire double-layer fringe trim strip. (Refer to Quick Fringe directions on page 14.)

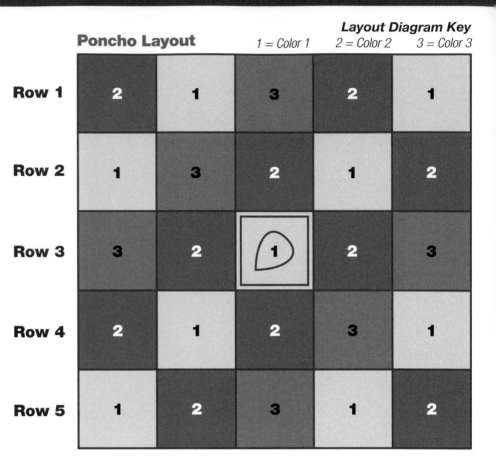

Poncho Layout

Layout Diagram Key
1 = Color 1   2 = Color 2   3 = Color 3

Row 1	2	1	3	2	1
Row 2	1	3	2	1	2
Row 3	3	2	1	2	3
Row 4	2	1	2	3	1
Row 5	1	2	3	1	2

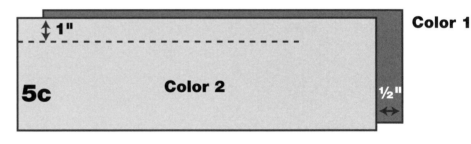

5c   1"   Color 2   Color 1   ½"

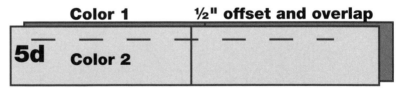

5d   Color 1   ½" offset and overlap   Color 2

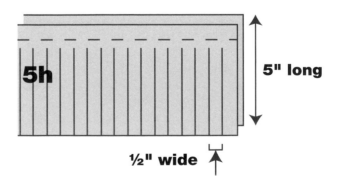

5h   5" long   ½" wide

6. Finish the poncho.

a. With right sides facing up and beginning on one long side edge of the poncho (do not begin at a corner), lay the edge of poncho over the 1" basted seamline of fringe trim, just covering the stitches.

b. Use blanket stitch B to attach the poncho and the double-layer fringe trim.

c. When you get to a corner, sink the needle in the poncho, spread open a fringe slit and pivot to "get around the corner."

d. As you get around the poncho, returning to the beginning spot, stop stitching approximately 2" before the beginning fringe.

e. Measure and cut remaining fringe the length necessary to abut fringe ends

f. Finish blanket-stitching poncho to the fringe.

g. Change to a regular 4mm-long straight stitch and topstitch ¼" away from blanket stitching.

h. Use appliqué scissors to trim excess fringe trim seam allowance close to topstitching.

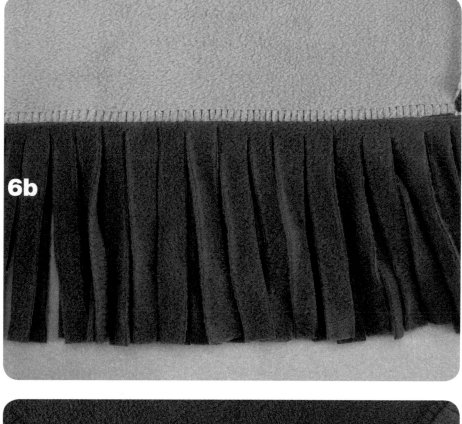

Dramatic Chenille Cape

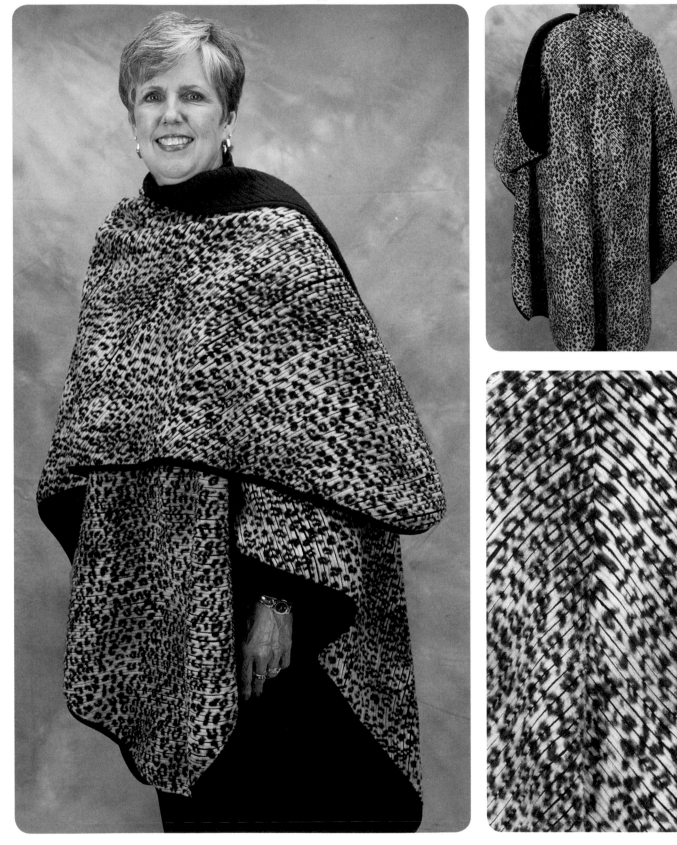

The first time this cape was displayed at International Quilt Market in Houston, it stopped people in the aisles because of its simplicity and because the chenille makes the fleece elegant and dramatic.

Then came the comment (from a quilter): "Wow! That's a lot of stitching."

My answer: "So is stippling a queen-size quilt." Quilter's reply: "I get your point."

There is a lot of plain stitching on this cape. A lot of simple stitching that produces a drop-dead gorgeous result—kind of like stippling a quilt!

This dramatic cape is simple to make. Time consuming, yes, but it is simple to sew.

It is basically rows and rows and rows of parallel straight stitching. Not difficult, just repetitive.

Obviously, I really took creative liberty including this project under the 90-minute title. It by no means is a "project in an evening," but it can easily be tackled in 90-minute increments.

I did not make this in one or even two evenings. I probably spent three or four evenings just stitching the chenille rows. I allocated two hours of straight stitching and one-and-a-half glasses of wine per session; two hours because although it's not mind-challenging, it does get boring and one-and-a-half glasses of wine because wine makes the two hours more enjoyable (and any more wine resulted in stitching lines that were neither particularly straight nor parallel)!

My time frame: I would estimate I spent six to seven hours chenille stitching, one hour slashing (Use the Olfa Chenille Cutter or electric scissors, as Omni Ministrips would be cumbersome to use in this setting.) and one hour construction. So, figure nine to 10 hours total.

Materials Needed

Fleece print*: 2½ yards
Fleece solid: 2½ yards
Lycra trim: 8 yards
Water-soluble pencil
Olfa Chenille Cutter or electric scissors

*Not suitable for one-way designs

nancy's note

Directions are given here for creating your own cape pattern. However, you could use one of the many commercial patterns offered at your favorite fabric store. If you do choose a commercial cape pattern, consider the following:

- *Choose one with a plain front opening and plain side openings.*
- *If it has squared corners, gently round them. (This will make applying the Cheater's Wrapped Edge binding much easier.)*
- *Add a center back seam, instead of cutting "on the fold." Besides making the chenille stitching manageable (you could never do the chenille stitching on such a huge expanse of fabric), it allows you to chevron the chenille channels down the center back for a dramatic effect.*

Directions

1. Cut print fleece down the center (lengthwise, between the selvages) to form two 30" x 90" pieces.

2. Repeat Step 1 with the solid fleece.

3. Arrange each 30" x 90" print fleece piece against the solid pieces, *wrong* sides together. Place cut edges together and selvages together. Have nap (if applicable) running the same direction on all pieces.

4. Refer to the accompanying illustration and use a water-soluble pencil to draw 45-degree angled lines (for chenille stitching guidelines) on the right side of the solid fleece.

> **a.** Draw these stitching guidelines so they will chevron at the center back.
>
> **b.** Draw parallel lines 6" apart. These lines will serve to help keep the multiple stitching lines straight.

5. Stitch the chenille lines ⅜" apart. The fleece layers will shift a little during stitching. These uneven edges will be cut off when the cape sections are cut. Do not slash chenille stitching yet. (Refer to Chenille Yardage Steps 1 and 2 directions on page 23.)

6. Cut the two chenille-stitched pieces to 28" x 88" each. (This will neaten the uneven shifted layers. Don't worry if your chenille-stitched pieces don't quite give you enough room to cut to this size. Perhaps your fleece was a little narrower than 60" to begin or your layers shifted a lot during the stitching process. Cut your two pieces into equal rectangles as close to these dimensions as possible. This is a cape without any critical fit concerns, but the left and right side must be the same size.)

7. Refer to the accompanying illustration and take *one* chenille-stitched rectangle and cut the center front opening and neck edge. Round both of the front corners and outer back corner only. (Pay close attention and double-check to ensure your cutting matches the illustration. You want the chevron at the center back to point towards the back neck and flare out to the side hem.)

8. Lay the cut-out chenille-stitched rectangle on top of the other rectangle, print sides together. Use the cut-out rectangle as a cutting guide and cut the other rectangle to match. *Important: Make sure chenille lines chevron at center back.*

9. Slash open the chenille channels. (Refer to Chenille Yardage step 3b directions on page 24, or use electric scissors.)

10. Sew center back pieces, right sides together, using a ¼" seam allowance. (Don't attempt to "match" chenille channels. Trust me—it's a futile effort and they end up looking matched anyway!)

11. Fold the cape in half, matching front hem to back hem. Using the front hem as a cutting guide, round the back hem side corners.

12. Finish the entire outer edge with Cheater's Wrapped Edge. Use a ⅜" seam allowance. (Refer to Cheater's Wrapped Edge directions on page 30 and Splicing Trim directions on page 31, if necessary.)

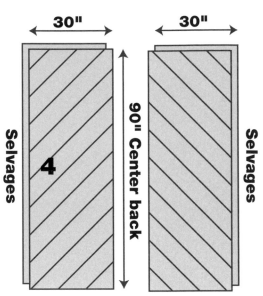

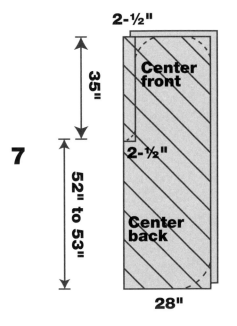

Bias Patchwork Scarf and Coordinating Hat

The lapped edge technique makes this scarf very easy to sew. Because the seams are overlapped, both the front and back of the scarf look the same.

Materials Needed
Scarf and Hat Combined
Color 1 fleece (black): ⅝ yard
Color 2 fleece (royal): ⅝ yard
Wash-Away Wonder Tape
Decorative wave blade
Pattern tracing paper

Scarf Directions

1. Refer to the accompanying illustration and draw a scarf pattern piece on pattern tracing paper as follows:

> **a.** Draw a 6½" x 21" rectangle.

> **b.** Mark dot A on the left side, 6½" below the top edge.

> **c.** Draw a diagonal line from dot A to the upper right corner.

> **d.** Mark dot B on the right side, 6½" above the lower edge.

> **e.** Draw a diagonal line from dot B to the lower left corner.

> **f.** Cut on the diagonal lines. Discard corner triangles.

> **g.** Mark the pattern piece as "right side."

2. Use the decorative wave blade to cut five 6½" x 21" rectangles from Color 1 fleece and four 6½" x 21" rectangles from Color 2 fleece. (The 21" height is on the straight of grain. The greater stretch is in the 6½" width.)

3. Layer scarf pattern on top of fleece rectangle, both with right sides up. It is very important that the fabric be a single-layer with right side facing up and the scarf pattern piece be right-side up. Otherwise, the bias cuts will not align for the scarf.

4. Cut the upper and lower diagonal edges, following the pattern.

5. Repeat Steps 3 and 4 on all Color 1 and Color 2 fleece rectangles.

6. Create the scarf from left to right, with right sides facing up, as follows:

> **a.** Place Wash-Away Wonder Tape on the long left edge of a Color 2 patch.

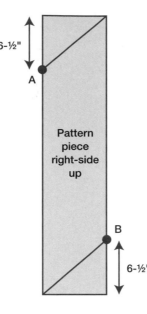

1
Pattern piece right-side up

6-½"

A

B

6-½"

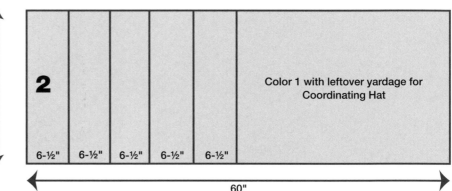

2

21"

6-½" 6-½" 6-½" 6-½" 6-½"

Color 1 with leftover yardage for Coordinating Hat

60"

PATTERN RIGHT SIDE UP
FABRIC RIGHT SIDE UP
3
RIGHT SIDE

6

> **b.** Lap a Color 1 patch ⅜" and adhere to the basting tape.

> **c.** Stitch using a straight or serpentine stitch, as desired.

> **d.** Continue lapping, adhering and stitching patches. Alternate colors, beginning and ending with a Color 1 patch.

7. Use the decorative wave blade to retrue edges, if necessary.

Hat Directions

1. Use the decorative wave blade to cut two 6" x 20" rectangles each from Color 1 and Color 2 fleece, with the greater stretch going in the 6" width.

2. Place Wash-Away Wonder Tape on the left edges of Color 2, Color 1 and Color 2 rectangles, with right sides facing up, as shown in the accompanying photo. Begin tape 8" below the top edge of each rectangle.

3. Work from left to right, lapping ⅜", to adhere and stitch a Color 1 rectangle to a Color 2 rectangle, leaving the top 8" unstitched. Continue by adding a Color 1 to the Color 1-2 piece and finishing with a Color 2 rectangle added to the Color 1-2-1 piece.

4. Use the decorative wave blade to make ½" x 8" fringe-cuts in the unstitched 8" areas of each hat section.

5. Bring long edges of the stitched hat right sides together (traditional seam), to form a tube and sew the center back seam using a ¼" seam allowance, leaving the top 8" unstitched.

6. Fold under a 3" hem and topstitch in place.

7. Gather hat at the beginning of the fringe-cuts and tie securely with a narrow fleece strip.

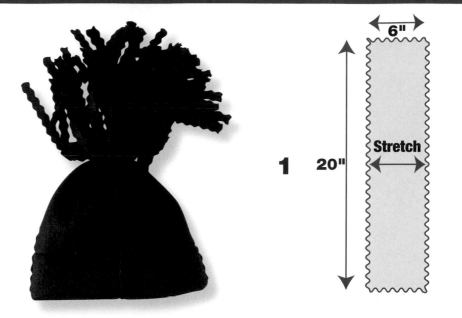

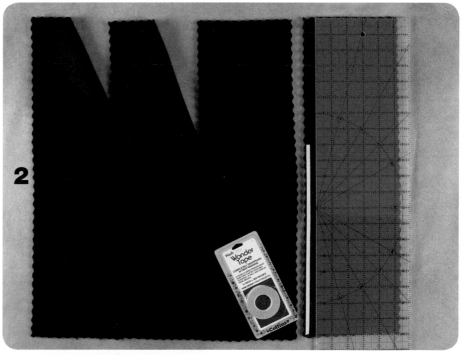

nancy's note

Try on the hat. If you would like a snugger fit, re-stitch the center back seam taking a deeper seam allowance.

Striped Scarf

This fast-and-fun scarf is accented by exposed seam allowances trimmed with scalloped rotary-cut edges. You'll spend more time choosing your colors than you will sewing the scarf!

Materials Needed
Color 1 fleece: ¼ yard
Color 2 fleece: ¼ yard
Color 3 fleece: ¼ yard
Decorative scallop blade

Directions

1. Cut two 3" x 60" strips from each of the three fleece colors using the straight blade rotary cutter.

2. Sew one long edge of a Color 1 strip to a Color 2 strip, *wrong* sides together, using a ½" seam allowance. (Don't worry if the short ends don't match. They will be trimmed later.)

3. Trim ¼" from the exposed seam allowance using the decorative blade. (This results in a double-layered scallop exposed seam allowance.)

4. Repeat Steps 2 and 3, stitching the just-sewn Color 1-2 strip to a Color 3 strip.

5. Repeat Steps 2 through 4 to finish the scarf.

6. Trim all outer edges of the scarf with the decorative scallop blade.

nancy's note

Caution: *The scallop rotary cutting blade produces two decorative edges, depending upon how you attach the blade to the handle. (Refer to Rotary Cutters directions on page 12.)*

Braided Scarf

This scarf can be made from three solids, three prints or any combination of solids and prints. It is so simple, yet trendy, that it would be a great project for young girls to make.

Materials Needed

Color 1 fleece (print or solid): 1/8 yard
Color 2 fleece (print or solid): 1/8 yard
Color 3 fleece (print or solid): 1/8 yard
Tube turner, loop turner or string and safety pin

Directions

1. Cut each fleece piece 4½" x 60". (If one of your fleeces happens to be shorter than the others, cut all fleece pieces to the same length.)

2. Fold each piece in half lengthwise, right sides together, to create 2¼" x 60" folded pieces.

3. Use a ¼" seam allowance to sew each 2½" x 60" piece along the long raw edge, starting and stopping 5" from each end.

4. Use a tube turner, loop turner or string with a large safety pin on the end to turn each tube right-side out.

5. Cut each unstitched 5" end into ½"-wide x 5"-long fringe-cuts. (Although I love the Quick Fringe technique, I didn't use it here.)

6. Cut off one fringe from two of the fringed tubes (to use as ties after braiding the scarf).

7. Finger-gather and pinch together the three scarf tubes at one end and use one of the cut-off fringe pieces to tie the tubes tightly together at the beginning of the fringe-cuts.

8. Braid the scarf loosely.

9. Repeat Step 7 at the other scarf end.

3

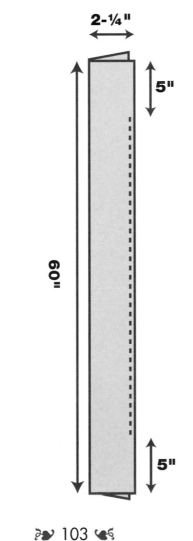

2-¼"

5"

60"

5"

Patriotic Scarf

The crisp red, white and blue color combination teamed with the gently waving stripes make it easy to be classy and patriotic at the same time. The double-sided star appliqués make both sides of the scarf the "right side."

Materials Needed

Pure white fleece: ⅜ yard
Red fleece: ⅓ yard
Bright navy fleece: ¼ yard
Wash-Away Wonder Tape
Fancy Fleece ruler
Star Template on pattern sheet

nancy's note

This is one of those simple projects that is so much easier when you take advantage of the right tools and notions. The Fancy Fleece ruler from June Tailor Inc. makes it simple to cut consistent wavy edges. And you can sew through Wash-Away Wonder Tape, so the wavy edges are easy to align and stitch.

Directions

Note: Fleece is right side facing up for all steps.

1. Cut:

- three 2½" x 60" wavy red stripes using the Fancy Fleece ruler
- two 2½" x 60" wavy white stripes using the Fancy Fleece ruler
- one 9" x 13" blue rectangle with straight edges

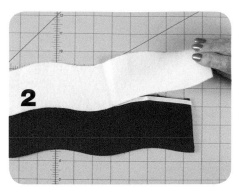

2. Place Wash-Away Wonder Tape on the right side of one red fleece along the upper wavy cut edge. (Since the paper backing is still adhered to the tape at this point, it will be a little stiff maneuvering the wavy edges. When you remove the paper backing from the tape it will lay flat.)

3. Remove paper backing.

4. Overlap a white stripe ⅜" on top of the red stripe, with right sides facing up and aligning the wavy edges.

5. Repeat Steps 2 through 4, resulting in a red-white-red-white-red scarf.

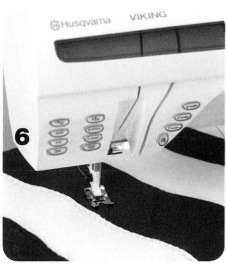

6. Place matching threads in the needle and bobbin and sew stripes together, stitching through the basting tape. Choose a multiple-stitch serpentine stitch (wavy snake-like stitch). Adjust the stitch width and length to complement the wavy cut edge of fleece.

7. Trim both short ends of the scarf, using the wavy edge of the Fancy Fleece ruler to maintain the "waving in the breeze" feeling.

8. Lay the wavy short end of scarf slightly overlapping the blue patch, with right sides facing up, and cut the blue patch using the wavy edge of the scarf as a guide. (The blue patch will be wider than scarf.)

9. Place Wonder Tape on the right side of striped scarf end. Overlap, adhere, and stitch blue patch.

10. Us the Fancy Fleece ruler to trim the blue patch side and bottom edges to match the scarf edges.

11. Cut six white fleece 5" squares for appliqué patches.

12. Use Clover Mesh Transfer Canvas and a water-soluble pencil to draw three white stars on the right side of three white patches, using the Star Template in the pattern insert. (Refer to Mesh Transfer Canvas directions on page 11.)

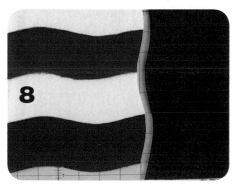

13. Stitch the double-sided appliqué stars onto the blue patch and trim. (Refer to the main project photo for suggested star placement and the Double-Sided Blunt-Edge Appliqué directions on page 15.)

Checkerboard Fleece Blanket

Finished size: 48" x 60"

This is the perfect lap blanket for the family room or game room.
Reverse Appliqué makes it easy to get the checkerboard effect.

Materials Needed
Main fleece: 1-⅓ yards
Contrast fleece: 1-⅓ yards
Appliqué scissors (pointed or round-tipped)

Directions

1. Cut both fleece layers into 48" x 60" pieces.

2. Place fleece layers *wrong* sides together (finished position). Stitch a ½" seam allowance on both long sides and a 4" seam allowance at both short ends.

3. Stitch a line from side seam to side seam 2½" away from the first seamline on one short end. Stitch another line in the same manner another 2½" toward the center. Repeat this step on the other end of the double-layer blanket.

4. Refer to the accompanying illustration and stitch perpendicular lines (cross seams) every 2½" to create 2½" stitched squares. (To allow for potential square size variations that naturally occur when sewing on a stretch fabric, stop to measure the remaining space when you get five squares from the end. Alter the remaining square sizes slightly, as necessary, to end up with visually consistent squares.)

5. Use appliqué scissors to trim just the top layer (main color) from within every other square to reveal the contrast color and form a checkerboard pattern.

6. Turn the blanket over and use appliqué scissors to trim just the top layer (contrast fleece) from the opposite double-layered squares. (This will form a checkerboard pattern on the contrast side of the blanket.)

7. Make ½" x 4" fringe-cuts along the short ends of the blanket. (Refer to Quick Fringe directions on page 14.)

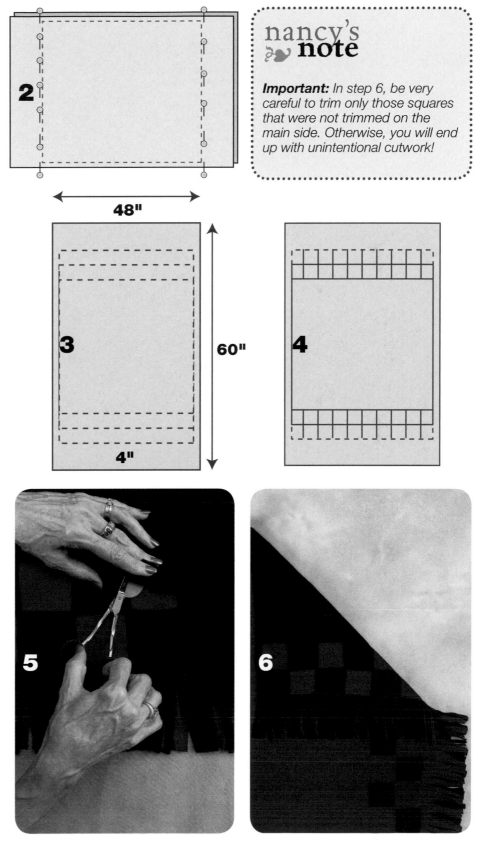

nancy's note

Important: *In step 6, be very careful to trim only those squares that were not trimmed on the main side. Otherwise, you will end up with unintentional cutwork!*

Skin Print Blanket and Shaggy Pillows

There are a lot of striking animal prints and skin prints on the market that, teamed with black, would make this dramatic blanket and pillow set. But don't overlook other prints, especially plaids and foliage prints, for making this threesome.

Materials Needed
Throw (54" x 60")
Fleece print: 1½ yards
18mm rotary cutter
Blanket (60" x 72")
Fleece print: 2 yards
Pillow set
Fleece print: ½ yard
Fleece solid: ⅔ yard
2 16" pillow forms
Appliqué scissors (pointed or round-tipped)

Throw/Blanket Directions

1. Cut the fleece print into a 54" x 60" (throw) or 60" x 72" (blanket) rectangle .

2. Cut away 5" squares from each corner.

3. Quick fringe the edges on all four sides, cutting the fringe 1" wide x 5" long. (Refer to Quick Fringe directions on page 14.)

4. Use 18mm rotary cutter to cut a tiny ¼" slit at the center bottom of each fringe.

5. Insert each fringe tip through the slit from the back and pull it through to the right side of the blanket. (Refer to Bunny Ears Blanket steps 5 and 6 on page 41.)

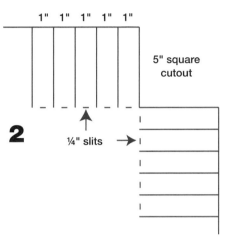

2

1" 1" 1" 1" 1"

5" square cutout

¼" slits →

Pillow Directions

The following cutting directions are for making the "set" of pillows, which includes a Four-Square Pillow and a Patchwork Pillow. Note that all seams in both types of pillows are sewn using a 1" seam allowance.

Cutting

1. Cut from solid fleece:
- two 10" squares
- two 18" squares
- one 6" x 60" strip

2. Cut from print fleece:
- two 10" squares
- one 6" x 60" strip

Solid Fleece Cutting Diagram

24"	10" square	10" square	18" square	18" square
	6" x 60" strip			

60"

Four-Square Pillow Construction

1. Cut and remove 1" squares from all four corners of the solid 10" squares, the print 10" squares and one 18" solid square.

2. Pin and stitch one print square to one solid square, *wrong* sides together.

3. Pin and stitch one solid square to one print square, *wrong* sides together.

4. Pin and stitch the print-solid pair (Step 2) to the solid-print pair (Step 3), *wrong* sides together.

5. Place the four-square pillow front on top of the 18" solid square back, *wrong* sides together. Sew together on three sides, leaving one side open for pillow form insertion.

6. Insert pillow form.

7. Stitch remaining side.

8. Cut exposed seam allowances into fringe ½" wide x 1" long, being careful not to cut the stitching lines.

This pillow design uses the two 10" solid squares, two 10" print squares and one 18" solid square.

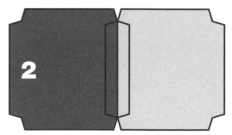

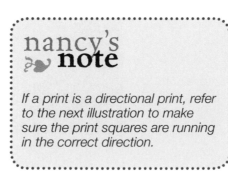

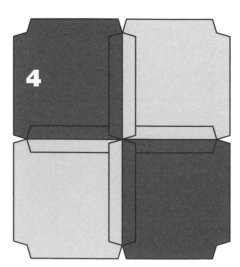

nancy's note

If a print is a directional print, refer to the next illustration to make sure the print squares are running in the correct direction.

Patchwork Pillow Construction

1. Cut the 6" x 60" solid strip into four 6" x 10" rectangles.

2. Cut 6" x 60" print strip into four 6" x 10" rectangles.

3. Cut and remove 1" squares from all four corners of all the rectangles and the 18" solid square, just as in Step 1 of the Four-Square Pillow Construction.

4. Pin and stitch one print rectangle to one solid rectangle, *wrong* sides together, just as in Step 2 of the Four-Square Pillow Construction. Repeat three times to make a total of four print-solid pairs.

5. Pin and stitch one print-solid pair to a second print-solid pair, offsetting the direction of the rectangles, to create the upper pillow front.

6. Repeat Step 5 for the lower pillow front.

7. Pin and stitch the upper pillow front to the lower pillow front to create full pillow front.

8. Finish pillow as in Steps 5 through 8 of the Four-Square Pillow Construction.

This pillow design uses one 6" x 60" solid strip, one 6" x 60" print strip and one 18" solid square.

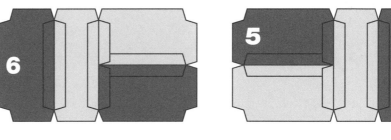

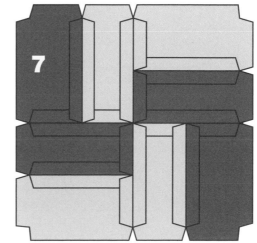

Winter Scene Throw and Pillows

This refreshing winter-themed print offers an easy way to do a quick "season change" in your home décor. When choosing a print to make a coordinating set like this, look for a print that offers at least two to four solid colors that you can incorporate into accent pillows. You also want a print that offers motifs suitable for appliqué embellishment on the pillows. (The motifs pulled from this print lend a quilt block flavor to the pillow.) The single-layer throw is quick-fringed on four sides. (On a slow day, it might take you 10 minutes to make it.) The pillows, like most of the pillows featured throughout this book, are simple envelope-style pillows. You can make this threesome in 90 minutes.

Materials Needed
Throw (54" x 60")
Fleece print*: 1½ yards
Blanket (60" x 72")
Fleece print*: 2 yards
Pillows
Fleece print: Enough yardage for appliqué motifs
Fleece solids and pillows forms: Refer to page 33 and 35 for yardage needed

*Purchase extra yardage for pillow appliqués

Throw/Blanket Directions

1. Cut the fleece print into a 54" x 60" rectangle (throw) or 60" x 72" rectangle (blanket).

2. Cut away 4" squares from all four corners.

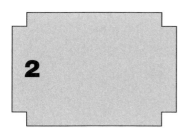

3. Quick fringe the edges on all four sides, cutting the fringe a generous ½" wide x 4" long. (Refer to Quick Fringe directions on page 14.)

Pillow Directions

1. Study your fleece print and decide what motifs you want to feature on the pillow fronts. Some allover prints do not offer a defined motif, but that does not have to stop you from using that print in pillow appliqués. (Refer to the Southwest Blanket and Pillows on page 114 for directions on how to make your own appliqué motifs.)

2. Refer to Pillow Construction and Fat Piping Edge Finish directions on pages 33-35 for cutting and sewing directions.

3. Refer to the Blunt-Edge Appliqué Cut-and-Stitch Method on page 16 for appliqué directions.

nancy's note

When making two pillows, you can make them both the same or different sizes—whatever suits your taste. The appliqué motifs will somewhat dictate the pillow sizes. Allow a minimum of 1½" space between the edge of an appliqué and the Fat Piping seam. (3" from beginning cut edge of pillow front.) Some appliqués will look better with a lot of surrounding space. Each print is different. I decided on a 16" and 18" pillow for this twosome. Both are appropriate sizes for use as couch accents. I felt the motifs would look best resting completely on the top part of the pillow, rather than going over the crest of the pillow toward the piping seam. So that influenced my decision not to choose a 14" pillow.

Southwest Blanket and Pillows

This was an interesting print to work with because it doesn't offer any obvious appliqué motifs, but it offers a lot of "potential" appliqués. And it has many solid colors to pull out for use in accent pillows. So, it was just a matter of playing with the print until a brainstorm hit.

You'll notice that simple is better—and easier. The appliqué motif does not have to be a great work of art. Let the print dictate the direction to take.

The single-layer throw is quick-fringed on two sides and embellished with pony beads to add to the southwest flavor of the print. I chose to make two 16" pillows embellished with "made-up" appliqués taken from the blanket print and then tossed in a 14" pillow made from a coordinating fleece print. Choose whatever pillow sizes best complement your appliqué choices.

Materials Needed

Throw (54" x 60")
Fleece print*: 1½ yards
Size US 9/1.25mm crochet hook or Fasturn
6mm x 9mm pony beads: 2 gross (optional)

Blanket (60" x 72")
Fleece print*: 2 yards

Pillows
Fleece print: Enough yardage for the appliqué motifs
Fleece solids and pillows forms: Refer to pages 33 and 35 for yardage needed
18 pony beads

*Purchase extra yardage for pillow appliqués

Throw/Blanket Directions

1. Cut the fleece print into a 54" x 60" (throw) or 60" x 72" (blanket) rectangle.

2. Quick fringe the edges on the two opposite sides that are most appropriate for your chosen print, cutting the fringe a generous ½" to ⅝" wide x 5" long. If there is not an "obvious" side to fringe, make the fringe-cuts on the shorter sides. (Refer to Quick Fringe directions on page 14.)

3. Optional: Place beads on fringe-cuts and tie to secure.

　　a. Stack a few pony beads on a small (US9/1.25mm) metal crochet hook or the metal pigtail of a Fasturn hook.

　　b. Hook a fringe end and slide a bead onto the fringe.

　　c. Tie a single knot at the fringe end and slide the bead down to the knot.

Pillow Directions

As stated earlier, this fleece print did not offer obvious motifs to cut out for appliqués, but it offered a lot of "potential." My plan of attack? First, I looked to find what solid colors I wanted to incorporate for the pillow base and trim. Then, I started working on appliqué designs for each of the pillows as follows.

First Pillow

1. Cut some stripes directly from the fleece print.

2. Arrange stripes on the pillow front until you like the balance.

3. Edgestitch the bands in place. (Refer to the Blunt-Edge Appliqué Cut-and-Stitch Method on page 16.)

4. Refer to Pillow Construction and Fat Piping Edge Finish directions on pages 33 and 30 for cutting and sewing directions.

Second Pillow

1. Cut a square from print fleece, making the square size complementary to your pillow front size. (There is no hard-and-fast rule here. It's just a matter of your personal taste.)

2. Fold the square point-to-point to create two triangles and finger-press the fold.

3. Reopen the square and using a rotary cutter, cut on the finger-pressed crease to create two triangles.

4. Position the triangle appliqués in place, as shown in the photo, and blanket stitch them onto the pillow front.

5. Cut three ⅜" x 12" strips.

6. Fold each strip in half to find the midpoint.

7. Machine-tack the strip midpoints to the middle of the pillow.

8. Add three pony beads to each strip, as in Step 3 of the Blanket/Throw Directions.

9. Refer to Pillow Construction and Fat Piping Edge Finish directions on page 33 for cutting and sewing directions.

Third Pillow

1. Refer to Pillow Construction and Fat Piping Edge Finish directions on page 33 for cutting and sewing directions.

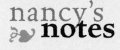

nancy's notes

🦢 *Cut fringe a little wider than ½" so it doesn't get distorted when you're beading the ends. Fringe-cuts, especially those made on the crossgrain, will stretch when pulled through the pony beads.*

🦢 *For an interesting effect, vary the number of beads on the fringe-cuts, or alternate bead colors.*

🦢 *Caution: Don't use beaded fringe on items that will be around babies or toddlers. Busy fingers and curious minds could result in beads pulled off and swallowed.*

1

2

3

Jaguar Blanket and Coordinating Pillows

Team a print with a coordinating solid and you have the makings of a quick home décor change. The pillows are a simple envelope style, so you can change them easily as the season change.

It's obvious that I love this print. I wore this print in a jacket on my More Polar Magic book cover, and I chose it again for this threesome. This blanket is "eco-friendly." The double-layer blanket allows you to turn down the thermostat and still ward off the autumn chill. The dramatic jaguar faces offer perfect embellishment opportunities: dramatic reverse appliqué on the blanket, blunt edge appliqué on one pillow and chenille texturing on the companion pillow.

This coordinating set could have just as easily featured a sports print, a scenic, a floral or other nature prints. All that is required is a coordinating solid color and a relatively simple-shaped motif for the appliqués.

Materials Needed
Add Blanket and Pillows needs together.

Throw (54" x 60")
Print fleece: 1½ yards
Coordinating solid fleece: 1½ yards
Blanket (60" x 72")
Print fleece: 2 yards
Coordinating solid fleece: 2 yards
Appliqué Pillow*
Solid fleece (pillow front and back): ⅝ yard
Contrast fleece (for appliqué and trim): ⅛ yard for
trim plus yardage as needed for appliqué
16" pillow form
Chenille Pillow*
Print fleece: ¾ yard (⅛ yard more than technically
needed to allow for making the chenille texture)
Solid color fleece: 1 yard
18" pillow form
*For different pillow sizes, refer to pages 33 and 35.
Remember for the chenille pillow to add ⅛ yard more
than required for the various sizes.

Throw/Blanket Directions

1. Cut both the fleece print and the fleece solid into a 54" x 60" rectangle (throw) or 60" x 72" rectangle (blanket).

2. Place the blanket layers wrong side together and pin to secure.

3. Place pins at each "to-be-fringed" side of the blanket, 3" to 5" from the edge, depending upon how long you want the fringe to be.

    a. If the print dictates which ends should be fringed (by design, by direction, by border, etc.), then fringe those opposing sides.

    b. If the print does not dictate a specific end, fringe the shorter sides.

4. Sew the blanket layers together, stitching the "unfringed" sides with a ½" seam allowance. Sew the to-be-fringed ends with a 3" to 5" seam allowance (equal to the fringe length).

5. Using a rotary cutter, trim the blanket edge close to the long unfringed seamline, extending the cut all the way to both ends of the blanket.

6. Quick fringe the ends, cutting the fringe ½" x 3 to 5" long. (Refer to Quick Fringe directions on page 14.)

7. Choose which prints you want to highlight with Reverse Appliqué. (Refer to Reverse Appliqué directions on page 20.)

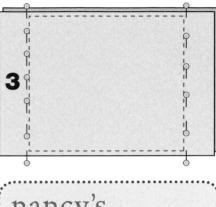

3

nancy's note

When using an allover print with many motifs to potentially choose, it is sometimes difficult to decide which motifs to stitch around to get a balanced look on the reverse (solid) side. I find it helpful to lay my pinned-together double-layer project on the floor, print side facing up, and place pieces of paper on the motifs I intend to stitch and trim. I can easily move the papers around until I get a balanced look. Then, I pin the papers in place so I can tell which are the "chosen motifs" when I get to the sewing machine.

Jaguar Appliqué Pillow

1. Refer to Pillow Construction and Fat Piping Edge Finish directions on page 33 for cutting and sewing directions.

2. Refer to the Blunt-Edge Appliqué Stitch-and-Cut Method on page 17 for appliqué directions.

nancy's note

You can mix and match pillow sizes according to what fits your print best. I chose a 16" pillow size for the appliquéd pillow. The size of the single jaguar face looked best on that size. I liked the drama of the chenille jaguar offered, so I chose a larger, 18" pillow size for that coordinating pillow.

Jaguar Chenille Pillow

1. From print fleece, cut one 26" square pillow front.

2. From solid fleece, cut:
- one 26" square pillow front
- two 19-½" x 13-¾" pillow half-backs
- two 4" x 60" trim strips

3. Chenille the pillow front. (Refer to Chenille Yardage directions on page 23.)

4. Trim the chenilled pillow front to 19-½" square.

5. Refer to Pillow Construction and Fat Piping Edge Finish directions on page 33 for sewing directions.

The simplicity of the black pillow top appliquéd with a jaguar face complements the allover jaguar print of the blanket.

Add chenille texture to a print, and all of a sudden your pillow adds texture as well as drama to your couch decor.

Appliquéd Tree Blanket

Team earthy colors with blanket-stitched tree appliqués and blanket-stitched exposed seams, and you have a casual country-flavor home décor accent. Because fleece does not ravel, all the seaming and appliqué techniques are simple.

Materials Needed

Fleece main color 1 (taupe block): 1 yard
Fleece contrast color 2 (brown block): ⅔ yard
Fleece accent color 3 (sage appliqué and fringe): 1⅓ yards
Contrast-colored thread
Temporary spray adhesive
Appliqué scissors (pointed or round-tipped)
Tree Template on pattern sheet

Directions

1. Cut the fleece, as follows:

- 13 9" x 12" rectangles from the main color (taupe), with the 12" height on the straight-of-grain (direction of least stretch).
- 12 9" x 12" rectangles from the contrast color (brown), with the 12" height on the straight-of-grain (direction of least stretch).
- 13 tree appliqués from the accent color (sage)
- four 6" x 60" fringe strips from the accent color (sage)

9"

12" **1**

Stretch

2. Set up your machine.

a. Place black or contrast thread in the needle and bobbin.

b. Select a blanket stitch on your machine, setting the stitch dimensions for a minimum stitch of 4mm long and 4mm wide.

c. Touch the mirror-image (side-to-side) function on your machine to change the blanket stitch back and forth to accommodate your needs, seaming or appliqué.

nancy's note

Review the important information in both the Nancy's Note and Nancy's Hint in the Checkerboard Poncho directions on page 91.

3. Stitch appliqués.

a. Lightly spray the wrong side of tree appliqués with temporary adhesive spray. Adhere one appliqué to the center of each main color rectangle.

b. Stitch appliqués in place using blanket stitch B (explained in Nancy's Note on page 91). For the easiest and least noticeable beginning and ending, start stitching the appliqué at the upper left corner of tree trunk.

3b

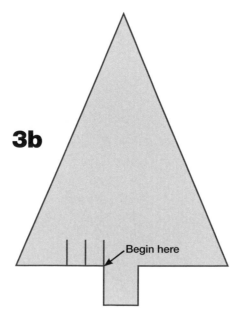

Begin here

4. Construct the blanket.

a. Construct Row 1 using blanket stitch A (in the Nancy's Note on page 91). Working from left to right, with wrong sides *always* together (all seam allowances will be exposed):

- Stitch Color 1 to Color 2.
- Stitch Color 1-2 pair to next C1.
- Follow the Blanket Layout diagram to finish Row 1.

b. Rows 2 through 5: Stitch rows as in Row 1, using the Blanket Layout as your color sequence guide.

c. Trim rows, as necessary, to neaten and retrue the edges.

d. Assemble the blanket by sewing the rows together using blanket stitch A. With *wrong* sides *always* together (all seam allowance will be exposed) and matching seams:

- Sew the bottom of Row 1 to the top of Row 2.
- Continue in the same manner for remaining rows.
- Trim outer edges of blanket, as necessary, to neaten and retrue the edges.

5. Fringe-cut the trim strips, cutting the fringe ½" wide x 5" long. (This leaves a 1" un-fringed header).

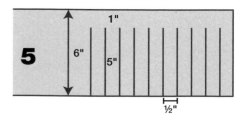

5 6" 1" 5" ½"

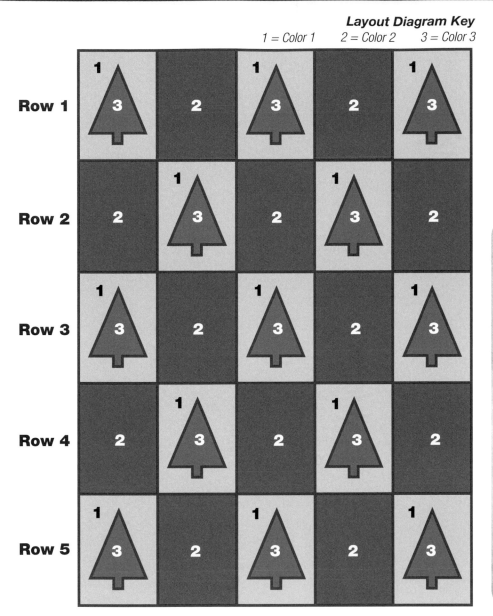

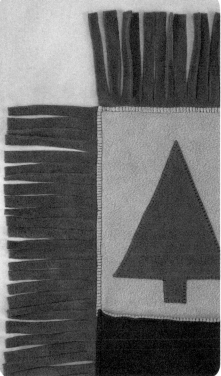

6. Attached the fringe trim, beginning at one corner, as follows:

a. Lay the edge of the blanket over the 1" header of the fringe strip, right sides facing up. Align the edge of the blanket a skimpy ¼" above the fringe-cuts.

b. Sew fringe to the blanket edge using blanket stitch B.

c. To be able to pivot around a corner, you want to have a fringe slit line up with the corner. As you get about 12" from the next corner, judge whether you will have a fringe slit line up. If not, slightly stretch the fringe trim so you have a fringe slit at the corner.

d. As you approach the corner, study the mechanics of the stitch and plan when to pivot the stitch. After you "make the turn," cut the fringe slit completely to the blanket corner point, to relieve any tension.

e. When you need to add the next fringe trim. Simply butt it next to the ending fringe trim and continue blanket stitching in place.

f. Use appliqué scissors to trim excess fleece from the fringe header on wrong side of blanket. Trim close to the stitching.

Chenille Leaf Throw

This lightweight throw brings a taste of autumn to your home. Change from earth-tone colors to soft spring pastels and change the appliqués from leaves to flowers and you have the perfect home accent to welcome spring. It's easy to have a variety of seasonal throws.

The leaves are Chenille Appliqué, the winding vine is a Chenille Strip, and the blanket is finished using the Cheater's Wrapped Edge technique. All quick and easy techniques taking advantage of fleece's nonravel characteristic.

Materials Needed

Main fleece: 1½ yards
Contrast fleece (for appliqués, vine and trim): ⅝ yard
Wash-Away Wonder Tape
Temporary spray adhesive
Decorative pinking blade
Full-Leaf and Half-Leaf Templates on pattern sheet

Directions

1. Cut the main fleece into a 54" x 60" throw, gently rounding the corners

2. Cut the contrast fleece, as follows:

- four 3" x 60" trim strips (edge finish)
- four ½" x 60" strips (vine strips), using the pinking blade rotary cutter

3. Cut the remaining contract fleece in half, forming two pieces 8" x 30".

4. Create the chenille appliqués and vine strips.

    a. With right sides facing up, place one 8" x 30" contrast piece on top of the other.

    b. Stitch the layers to make chenille yardage. (Refer to Chenille Yardage directions on page 23.)

    c. Use the Half-Leaf and Full-Leaf Templates on pattern sheet to cut out chenille leaf appliqués: 5 full leaves and 4 half leaves. (Refer to Chenille Appliqué steps 1 through 5 directions on page 25.) Set appliqués aside.

    d. Make two chenille strips for the vines and apply to the blanket in a random wandering arrangement. (Refer to Chenille Strips directions on page 27.)

5. Arrange chenille leaf appliqués, as desired. Edgestitch leaf appliqués in place. (Refer to Chenille Appliqué steps 6 and 7 on page 26.)

6. Splice trim strips together to make one long blanket edge trim strip. (Refer to Splicing Trim directions on page 31.)

7. Finish the throw with the Cheater's Wrapped Edge finish, stitching the trim strip to the outer edge of the blanket with a ½" seam allowance. (Refer to Cheater's Wrapped Edge directions on page 32.)

nancy's note

When working on a larger base piece, like a blanket, it is sometimes difficult to visualize where to place embellishments. I have found it helpful to spread the blanket on the floor and place the chenille strip vine and appliqués in various locations. I rearrange, as much as necessary, until I have a balance and feel that "looks right" to me. If it doesn't work the first time, walk away and come back with fresh eyes to rearrange again until you are happy with the look.

Christmas Tree Skirt

Combine the easy nature of fleece with the great prints and colors available on the market, and you have the makings of a quick-to-make eight-gore holiday tree skirt. Choose traditional colors or prints or go with the current trend. It's so easy to make that you can change the flavor every year! (And nowadays, you don't even have to restrict yourself to holiday prints!)

Materials Needed

Fleece print (nondirectional*): 1⅛ yards
Fleece solid: 1⅛ yards
Wash-Away Wonder Tape
Decorative scallop blade

*Note: To reduce fleece yardage requirements, we will be flip-flopping the tree skirt gore pattern pieces. If you are absolutely in love with a directional print, or choose a heavily napped solid where reversing the nap will be an issue, then purchase 1-¾ yards of that fleece and lay out the pattern pieces all going in the same direction.

Pattern Drafting Directions

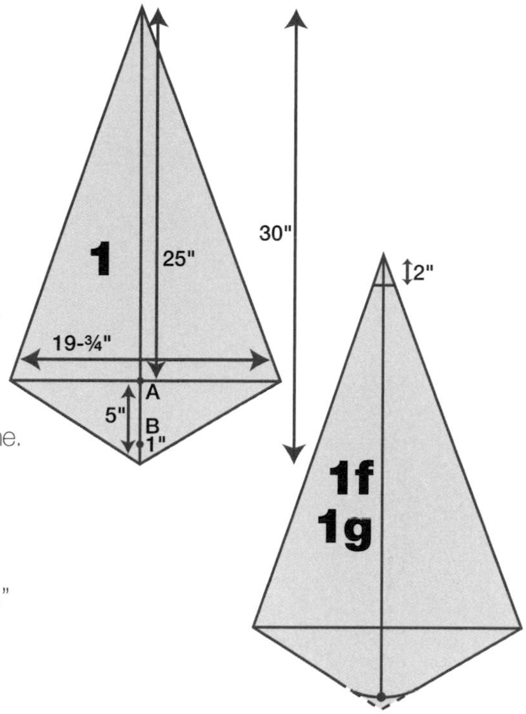

1. Refer to the accompanying illustrations and draw a pattern piece for the skirt gore as follows:

a. Draw a vertical line 30" high.

b. Mark dot A on the line 5" from the bottom and mark dot B 1" from the bottom.

c. Draw a horizontal line 19¾" long, intersecting the vertical line at dot A.

d. Draw angled line from the top of the vertical line to the ends of the horizontal line.

e. Draw angled lines from the bottom of the vertical line to the ends of the horizontal line. (You now have a kite-shaped piece.)

f. Gently round the bottom point. Use dot B as a guide for how much to "soften."

g. Trim 2" from the top point.

Tree Skirt Directions

1. Fold the print fleece and solid fleece in half so you will get four gores each, using just two pattern placements as shown in the accompanying illustration. Cut the gores using the scallop blade rotary cutter.

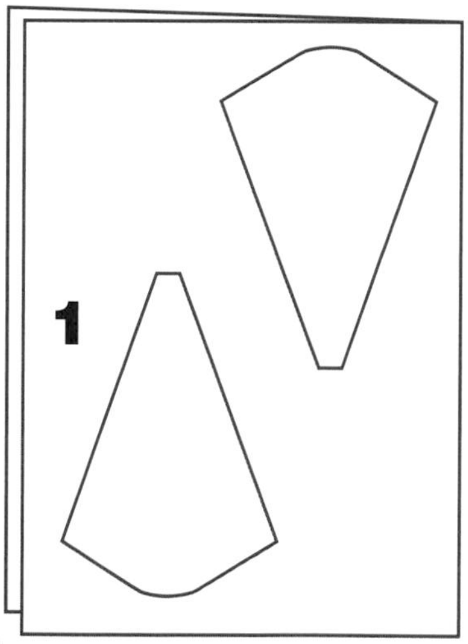

2. Place Wash-Away Wonder Tape along the long right edge of a solid-colored gore, right side facing up.

3. Build the tree skirt from left to right, with right sides always facing up.

a. Lap a print gore onto the basting-taped solid gore ⅜" and adhere in place. Begin at the lower flared edge, working up towards the narrow point.

b. Lap and adhere the next gore (solid) in place in the same manner. Do not worry if the narrow points don't quite match up. We will trim later, as needed.

c. Continue lapping and adhering gores, alternating prints and solids.

4. Sew the taped gores together using a serpentine stitch (or comparable wavy stitch). Lengthen and widen stitch, as necessary, to complement the scalloped edge.

5. Use the decorative scallop blade to trim the center top area to be even, as necessary.

nancy's caution

Be very careful when cutting, to make sure you are getting the scallop cut edge. (Refer to Rotary Cutters directions on page 12.)

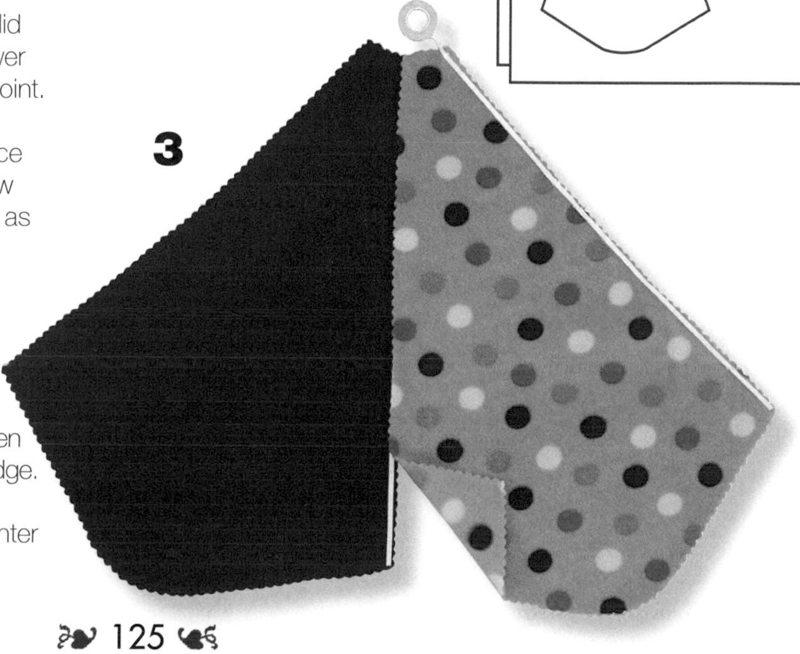

Contributors

Clover Needlecraft, Inc.
Sewing and quilting notions, cutting tools and specialty products
13438 Alondra Blvd.
Cerritos, CA 90703
E-mail: cni@clover-usa.com
Web: www.clover-usa.com

David Textiles, Inc.
Ask for Nordic® fleece at your favorite local retailer
1920 S. Tubeway Ave.
City of Commerce, CA 90040
Web: www.davidtextilesinc.com

Frank Edmunds & Co.
Quality wood products, including quilt rack featured on page 122
6111 S. Sayre
Chicago, IL 60638
Phone: 800-447-3516
Fax: 773-586-2783
E-mail: info@frankedmunds.com
Web: www.frankedmunds.com

Husqvarna Viking Sewing Machines
Manufacturer of precision sewing and embroidery machines
31000 Viking Parkway
Westlake, OH 44145
Phone: 800-358-0001
E-mail: info@husqvarnaviking.com
Web: www.husqvarnaviking.com

June Tailor
Cutting tools, sewing and quilting notions and related products
P.O. Box 208
Richfield, WI 53076
Phone: 800-844-5400
E-mail: customerservice@junetailor.com
Web: www.junetailor.com

Krause Publications
Publisher of this and other quality hobby-oriented and how-to books, including sewing, quilting, machine embroidery and other craft titles
700 E. State St.
Iola, WI 54990
Phone: 888-457-2873
Web: www.krausebooks.com

Olfa-North America
Precision cutting tools
5500 N. Pearl St., Suite 400,
Rosemont, IL 60018
Phone: 800-962-6532
Fax: 800-685-3950
Web: www.olfa.com

Prym Consumer USA
Sewing, quilting cutting and craft-related tools and notions, including Omnigrid and Omnigrip brand rotary cutting rulers and tools and Collins notions
P.O. Box 5028
Spartanburg, SC 29304
Web: www.dritz.com

Sulky of America
Manufacturer of threads, stabilizers and spray adhesives
P.O. Box 494129
Port Charlotte, FL 33949-4129
Phone: 800-874-4115 (to obtain a mail-order source)
E-mail: info@sulky.com
Web: www.sulky.com

Rowenta
Manufacturer of steamers and irons
196 Boston Ave.
Medford, MA 02155
Phone: 781-396-0600
Web: www.rowenta.com

The Crowning Touch
Quilting and sewing supplies and notions
3859 S. Stage
Medford, OR 97501
Phone: 800-729-0280
Fax: 541-772-5106
E-mail: support@crowning-touch.com
Web: www.crowning-touch.com

The Snap Source
Large range of colorful, long-prong snaps and The SnapSetter snap-attaching products
P.O. Box 99733
Troy, MI 48099-9733
Phone: 800-725-4600
Fax: 248-280-1140
Web: www.snapsource.com

Additional Resources
Catalogs and Web Sites

Annie's Attic
Phone: 800-582-6643
Web: www.anniesattic.com

Clotilde LLC
Phone: 800-772-2891
Web: www.clotilde.com

Connecting Threads
Phone: 800-574-6454
Web: www.ConnectingThreads.com

Herrschners Inc.
Phone: 800-441-0838
Web: www.herrschners.com

Home Sew
Phone: 800-344-4739
Web: www.homesew.com

Keepsake Quilting
Phone: 800-438-5464
Web: www.keepsakequilting.com

Nancy's Notions
Phone: 800-833-0690
Web: www.nancysnotions.com

Supplies
Tools and Notions

EZ Quilting by Wrights
Web: www.ezquilt.com

Fabric Café
2973-C Highway 155 S.
Tyler, TX 75703
Phone: 903-509-5999
Fax: 903-509-5981
Web: www.fabriccafe.com

Faux Chenille by Nanette Holmberg
724 South 1100 East
Salt Lake City, UT 84105
Phone: 801-485-6806
Fax: 801-943-9826
E-mail: nannette@xmission.com
Web: www.fauxchenille.com

Fiskars Brands Inc.
Web: www.fiskars.com

Malden Mills Industries
Manufacturers of Polartec and Polarfleece fabrics
E-mail: polartec@maldenmills.com
http://www.polartec.com

Schmetz
Web: www.schmetz.com

Sewing Machine Manufacturers

Baby Lock
Web: www.babylock.com

Bernina of America
Web: www.berninausa.com

Brother
Web: www.brother-usa.com

Elna USA
Web: www.elnausa.com

Husqvarna Viking
Web: www.husqvarnaviking.com

Janome
Web: www.janome.com

Kenmore
Web: www.sears.com

Pfaff
Web: www.pfaffusa.com

Singer
Web: www.singerco.com

Tacony Corp.
Web: www.tacony.com

White
Web: www.whitesewing.com

explore more opportunities to create fantastic fleece garments